THE OFFICIAL ENGLAND ANNUAL 2021

Written by Andy Greeves
Designed by Chris Dalrymple

A Grange Publication

Printed in the EU.

ISBN: 978-1-913034-93-1

CONTENTS

WELCOME TO THE OFFICIAL ENGLAND ANNUAL 2021

In the words of England Men's Senior team manager Gareth Southgate, 2020 was "not the moment" for the Three Lions or Lionesses to "take centre-stage" as the world responded to the challenges of the COVID-19 pandemic. As a new season begins, we give thanks to our NHS and the millions of key workers who continue to be our national heroes.

During lockdown, Gareth told England fans that "when we play again as an England team, it will be at a time when not only our country but the rest of the world as well is on the road to recovery." Hopefully 2021 will be a time when we can all enjoy what the manager describes as the "beautiful distraction that football can bring."

All being well, the Three Lions will be competing at UEFA Euro 2020 this summer, after the tournament was postponed last year and rescheduled for 11 June to 11 July 2021. Wembley Stadium will host seven matches during the competition, including all of England's Group D matches as well as both semi-finals and the final. In readiness for the competition, we profile those players hoping to be involved, take a look back at past England European Championship matches and check out the Three Lions' Group D opponents.

We'll also take a look at the players which make up the Senior Women's squad - as they continue to prepare for UEFA Women's EURO 2022 - and discover what the Lionesses were up to during lockdown. There are other features, quizzes, games and plenty more besides to entertain England fans of all ages!

COME ON ENGLAND
#ThreeLions #Lionesses

EUROPEAN CHAMPIONSHIP CLASSICS - EURO STARS!

Following the rescheduling of UEFA Euro 2020 to the summer of 2021, Gareth Southgate's England will play their first Group D tournament match against Croatia at Wembley Stadium on 13 June 2021. In readiness for the big kick-off, we take a look back at a series of memorable Three Lions victories at past UEFA European Championships.

★ ENGLAND 2-0 SOVIET UNION

UEFA Euro 1968 - Third Place Play-Off
08 June 1968
Stadio Olimpico, Rome, Italy

England's first foray into the UEFA European Championships came back in 1968 as Sir Alf Ramsey's world champions headed to Italy for the four-team tournament. A semi-final defeat to Yugoslavia resulted in the Three Lions competing in the third-place play-off against the Soviet Union. Bobby Charlton gave Ramsey's team the lead six minutes before the half-time interval as he got on the end of a neat touch from Geoff Hurst before firing home from just outside the six-yard-box. Hurst wrapped up the victory on 63 minutes, as he rounded goalkeeper Yuri Pshenichnikov and tucked the ball into the back of the net.

England: Banks, Wilson, Labone, Moore (c), Hunter, Wright, B. Charlton, Peters, Stiles, Hurst, Hunt

Soviet Union: Pshenichnikov, Afonin, Banishevski, Byshovets, Yevryuzhikhin, Istomin, Kaplichni, Malofeev, Shesternev (c), Lenev, Logofet

★ ENGLAND 2-0 SCOTLAND

UEFA Euro 1996 - Group A
15 June 1996
Wembley Stadium, London

England had the honour of hosting the European Championships in 1996 as the tournament featured 16 nations for the first time. After a 1-1 draw with Switzerland in the opening match of the competition, the Three Lions took on Scotland in their second Group A fixture. After a goalless first-half, Alan Shearer gave England the lead eight minutes after the break.

With less than 15 minutes of the match remaining, Scotland were awarded a penalty when Tony Adams was adjudged to have fouled Gordon Durie in the England penalty area. David Seaman saved Gary McAllister's resulting spot-kick and moments later, Paul Gascoigne scored a memorable second goal for the Three Lions. Collecting a fine lofted pass from Darren Anderton, 'Gazza' flicked the ball over the head of defender Colin Hendry with his first touch before rifling a right-footed volley past Andy Goram in the Scottish goal with his second.

England: Seaman, Pearce (Redknapp 46, Campbell 85), Southgate, Adams (c), G. Neville, McManaman, Gascoigne, Ince (Stone 80), Anderton, Shearer, Sheringham

Scotland: Goram, Boyd, Hendry, Calderwood, McKimmie; Collins, McAllister (c), McCall, T. McKinlay (Burley 82), Durie (Jess 87), Spencer (McCoist 67)

★ ENGLAND 0-0 SPAIN

1

(England win 4-2 on penalties)
UEFA Euro 1996 - Quarter-final
22 June 1996
Wembley Stadium, London

After their quarter-final against Spain finished goalless following extra-time, England faced the drama of their first-ever penalty shootout at a European Championships. David Seaman saved efforts from Fernando Hierro and Miguel Angel Nadal in the shootout while Alan Shearer, David Platt, Stuart Pearce and Paul Gascoigne were all on target from 12 yards to seal a 4-2 spot-kick triumph. For Pearce in particular it was a sweet moment of redemption, following his miss in the World Cup semi-final shootout against Germany six years earlier.

England: Seaman, Pearce, Southgate, Adams (c), G. Neville, Anderton (Stone 109), Gascoigne, Platt, McManaman (Barmby 109), Sheringham (Fowler 109), Shearer

Spain: Zubizarreta (c), Abelardo, Alkorta (J. Lopez 72), Nadal, Sergi, Manjarin (Caminero 46), Amor, Hierro, Belsue, Salinas (Alfonso 46), Kiko

★ ENGLAND 4-1 NETHERLANDS

UEFA Euro 1996 - Group A
18 June 1996
Wembley Stadium, London

Terry Venables' England served up another classic performance at UEFA Euro 1996 as they thrashed the Netherlands in their final Group A fixture. A penalty from Alan Shearer gave the Three Lions a half-time lead, while Teddy Sheringham put them 2-0 up six minutes into the second period. Shearer and Sheringham both scored their second goals of the evening on 57 and 62 minutes respectively while Patrick Kluivert got a late consolation for the Dutch.

England: Seaman, Pearce, Southgate, Adams (c), G. Neville, McManaman, Gascoigne, Ince (Platt 68), Anderton, Shearer (Barmby 76), Sheringham (Fowler 77)

Netherlands: Van der Sar, Bogarde, Blind (c), Reiziger, Witschge (De Kock 46), Winter, Seedorf, R. de Boer (Cocu 73), Hoekstra (Kluivert 72), Bergkamp, Cruyff

★ ENGLAND 1-0 GERMANY

UEFA Euro 2000 - Group A
17 June 2000
Stade du Pays de Charleroi, Charleroi, Belgium

The Belgian city of Charleroi was the venue for England's Group A clash with Germany at UEFA Euro 2000, which saw Alan Shearer head the winner for the Three Lions on 53 minutes. The 1-0 triumph gave England their first competitive victory over Germany since the 1966 FIFA World Cup Final.

England: Seaman, G. Neville, Campbell, Keown, P. Neville, Beckham, Scholes (Barmby 71), Ince, Wise, Shearer (c), Owen (Gerrard 61)

Germany: Kahn (c), Matthaus, Babbel, Nowotny, Deisler (Ballack 72), Ziege, Hamann, Jeremies (Bode 78), Scholl, Jancker, Kirsten (Rink 70)

★ ENGLAND 3-0 SWITZERLAND

UEFA Euro 2004 - Group B
17 June 2004
Estadio Cidade de Coimbra, Coimbra, Portugal

Wayne Rooney briefly became the youngest goal scorer in the UEFA European Championship history when he scored twice in the Three Lions 3-0 triumph over Switzerland at UEFA Euro 2004 at the age of 18 years and 237 days – until his record was surpassed by Johan Vonlanthen, who scored for Switzerland against France just four days later at the age of 18 years and 141 days.

Rooney headed England in front after 23 minutes of their Group B encounter with Switzerland. After Bernt Haas was sent-off on the hour mark, Sven-Goran Eriksson's side extended their lead as a deflected Rooney effort beat Jorg Stiel in the Swiss goal. Steven Gerrard wrapped up the win as he forced Gary Neville's cross past Stiel with eight minutes of the 90 remaining.

England: James, Ashley Cole, Campbell, Terry, G. Neville, Scholes (Hargreaves 70), Lampard, Gerrard, Beckham (c), Rooney (Dyer 83), Owen (Vassell 72)

Switzerland: Stiel (c), Spycher, Muller, Murat Yakin, Haas, Wicky, Celestini (Cabanas 54), H. Yakin (Vonlanthen 84), Huggel, Frei, Chapuisat (Gygax 46)

★ ENGLAND 4-2 CROATIA

UEFA Euro 2004 - Group B
21 June 2004
Estadio da Luz, Lisbon, Portugal

Wayne Rooney's red-hot form at UEFA Euro 2004 continued as he bagged a brace in the Three Lions' final Group B fixture against Croatia. After going behind after just five minutes to Niko Kovac's close-range effort, Paul Scholes levelled for England five minutes before half-time. Scholes turned creator in added-time at the end of the first-half, flicking the ball into the path of Rooney who in turn lashed a shot past Tomislav Butina in the Croatian goal.

Rooney's second goal of the evening arrived on 68 minutes as he collected a pass from Michael Owen before scoring. Igor Tudor's 73rd-minute effort gave Croatia hope but Frank Lampard netted with eleven minutes left on the clock to seal England's passage to the quarter-finals of the competition.

England: James, Ashley Cole, Campbell, Terry, G. Neville, Scholes (King 70), Gerrard, Lampard (P. Neville 84), Beckham (c), Rooney (Vassell 72), Owen

Croatia: Butina, Simunic, R. Kovac (Mornar 46), Tudor, Simic (Srna 67), Rapaic (Olic 55), Zivkovic (c), Niko Kovac, Roso, Sokota, Prso

ENGLAND 3-2 SWEDEN

UEFA Euro 2012 - Group D
15 June 2012
Olympic Stadium, Kiev, Ukraine

A topsy-turvy UEFA Euro 2012 Group D match in Kiev eventually saw England claim their first competitive victory over Sweden. Andy Carroll's header gave the Three Lions a first-half lead but an own-goal from Glen Johnson and a header from Olof Mellberg put Sweden 2-1 up before the hour-mark. Theo Walcott levelled on 64 minutes before Danny Welbeck's clever match-winner – a back-flick finish from a Walcott cross on 78 minutes.

England: Hart, A. Cole, Lescott, Terry, Johnson, Young, Parker, Gerrard (c), Milner (Walcott 61), Welbeck (Oxlade-Chamberlain 90), Carroll

Sweden: Isaksson, M. Olsson, J. Olsson, Mellberg, Granqvist (Lustig 66), Elm (Wilhelmsson 81), Källström. Svensson, Larsson, Ibrahimović (c), Elmander (Rosenberg 79)

ENGLAND 1-0 UKRAINE

UEFA Euro 2012 - Group D
19 June 2012
Donbass Arena, Donetsk, Ukraine

England finished top of Group D after a 1-1 draw with France, a 3-2 victory over Sweden and a 1-0 triumph against tournament joint-hosts Ukraine in Donetsk. Wayne Rooney's strike three minutes into the second-half was enough for all three points as Roy Hodgson's side progressed to a quarter-final meeting with Italy.

England: Hart, A. Cole, Lescott, Terry, Johnson, Young, Parker, Gerrard (c), Milner (Walcott 70), Rooney (Oxlade-Chamberlain 87), Welbeck (Carroll 82)

Ukraine: Pyatov, Selin, Rakitskiy, Khacheridi, Gusev, Konoplyanka, Tymoshchuk (c), Garmash (Nazarenko 78), Yarmolenko, Milevskiy (Butko 77), Devic (Shevchenko 70)

ENGLAND 2-1 WALES

UEFA Euro 2016 - Group B
16 June 2016
Stade Bollaert-Delelis, Lens, France

Daniel Sturridge got a stoppage time winner for England at the end of their Group B encounter with Wales. Gareth Bale put the Dragons in front with a long-range free-kick three minutes before the half-time interval. Jamie Var dy came on as a half-time substitute for Raheem Sterling and made an instant impact, scoring an equaliser just 11 minutes later. As an evenly-fought clash looked set to end all square before Sturridge ran on to a loose-ball in the Wales penalty area and beat goalkeeper Wayne Hennessey at his near post.

England: Hart, Rose, Smalling, Cahill, Walker, Rooney (c), Dier, Dele, Sterling (Sturridge 46), Kane (Vardy 46), Lallana (Rashford 73)

Wales: Hennessey, Taylor, Davies, A. Williams (c), Chester, Gunter, Allen, Ledley (Edwards 67), Ramsey, Bale, Robson-Kanu (J. Williams 72)

GET READY FOR UEFA EURO 2020

Rescheduled to the summer of 2021 due to the COVID-19 pandemic, UEFA Euro 2020 kicks off on 11 June 2021 as Italy take on Turkey at the Stadio Olimpico in Rome.

Wembley Stadium will host seven matches during the 24-nation tournament, including England's three Group D matches. The first of these fixtures is against Croatia on 13 June (2pm kick-off) while their last group game is against Czech Republic on 22 June (8pm kick-off). England also have a group match at Wembley on 18 June at 8pm. More details on England's Group D opponents can be found on pages 24 and 25.

The winners of Group D will play their last-16 tie in Dublin on 29 June, while the runners up will head to Copenhagen a day earlier on 28 June. If England finish third, they could still progress and would play in either Budapest (28 June) or Glasgow (29 June). Both semi-finals of the competition will be held at Wembley on 6 and 7 July respectively while the final will also be hosted at the 'Home of Football' on 11 July.

GARETH SOUTHGATE THE ENGLAND YEARS

From a playing career that saw him win 57 caps for England between 1995 and 2004, to roles as manager of the Men's U21s and Men's Senior teams, Gareth Southgate's involvement with the Three Lions has spanned across four decades.

1995

After making 191 appearances and scoring 22 goals for his first professional club, Crystal Palace, Gareth Southgate departed Selhurst Park to sign for Aston Villa in the summer of 1995. Later that year the versatile player – who was converted into a centre-back during his time with the Villains – made his England debut as he came on as a substitute for Dennis Wise in a 1-1 friendly draw with Portugal at Wembley Stadium on 12 December.

1996

A few months after making his first England start in a 1-0 victory over Bulgaria at Wembley Stadium on 27 March, Gareth was selected in Terry Venables' 22-man squad for UEFA Euro 1996. The Watford-born defender started in all five of England's matches at the tournament. After the Three Lions' semi-final against Germany finished in a 1-1 draw after extra-time, Gareth's spot-kick was saved by goalkeeper Andreas Kopke as Die Mannschaft triumphed 6-5 in a penalty shoot-out and went on to win the competition, beating the Czech Republic in the final.

1998

Gareth played a major role in helping England reach the 1998 FIFA World Cup, as he made seven appearances in qualifying for the tournament. He played in two matches at the finals, including the round of 16 clash with Argentina in Saint-Etienne. Later that year, Gareth got the first of his two England goals during his international career in a 3-0 away win in Luxembourg.

2000

Gareth came on as a late substitute for Paul Scholes in England's Group A clash with Romania at UEFA Euro 2000, which marked an appearance at his third major tournament for England. He started in a 1-0 defeat to Germany on 7 October that year – the Three Lions' last match at the old Wembley Stadium.

2001

The summer of 2001 saw Gareth depart Aston Villa for Middlesbrough, for whom he went on to win the Football League Cup with in 2003 – the first major trophy in the club's history. Gareth made three appearances for England during 2001, including a substitute outing in the Three Lions' 4-0 victory over Mexico in May.

2002

Gareth was named in Sven-Goran Eriksson's 23-man squad for the 2002 FIFA World Cup but didn't feature in the tournament in Japan and South Korea. Fittingly for a former Aston Villa player, he won his 50th cap for England in a 1-1 draw with Portugal at Villa Park in September that year.

2003

Gareth scored his second and final goal for England in 2-1 friendly victory over South Africa in May. He made his last competitive appearance for the Three Lions in a 2-1 win against Slovakia a month later in a UEFA Euro 2004 qualifier.

2004

The year marked Gareth's final appearances for England. His penultimate game in a Three Lions shirt was a 1-1 draw with Portugal in February while his last-ever international appearance came in 1-0 defeat in Sweden the following month. He retired from playing club football in the summer of 2006, when he became Middlesbrough manager.

2013

After departing Middlesbrough in October 2009, Gareth's next football challenge saw him appointed as the Head Coach of England Men's U21s in August 2013. The Young Lions got off to a winning start under their new boss as they beat Moldova 1-0 in a European Championships qualifier the following month.

2015

England competed at the UEFA European U21 Championship in the Czech Republic, with Gareth's 23-man squad for the tournament including many members of his current Men's Senior team, such as Harry Kane, John Stones, Michael Keane, Jesse Lingard and Ruben Loftus-Cheek.

2016

Following the resignation of Sam Allardyce, Gareth was put in temporary charge of the Men's Senior team for fixtures against Malta, Slovenia, Scotland and Spain. He was appointed manager of the Men's Senior team in November 2016, as he put pen to paper on a four-year contract.

2017

A stoppage-time winner from Harry Kane saw England beat Slovenia 1-0 at Wembley Stadium in October to top their group and confirm their place at the 2018 FIFA World Cup.

2018

For the first time since 1990, England reached the semi-finals of the World Cup in Russia. The Three Lions' triumphed in a penalty shoot-out at the tournament for the first time, as they beat Colombia in the round of 16. There were also victories against Tunisia, Panama and Sweden prior to Gareth's team being beaten 2-1 after extra-time in their last-four tie against Croatia.

There was further success for England that year, as they topped their UEFA Nations League group to make it through to the inaugural finals of the competition.

2019

In recognition of England's efforts and achievements, Gareth was named as an Officer of the Most Excellent Order of the British Empire (OBE) in the New Year's Honours list. An extra-time defeat to the Netherlands followed by a 6-5 penalty shoot-out success over Switzerland in the UEFA Nations League Finals saw the Three Lions finish third at a major tournament for the first time since UEFA Euro 1968. Qualification to UEFA Euro 2020 was sealed with a spectacular 7-0 victory over Montenegro in November.

2020

Due to the outbreak of coronavirus, England were forced to cancel friendlies with Denmark, Italy, Austria and Romania while UEFA Euro 2020 was postponed until the summer of 2021. In an open letter to England fans, sent days before the country went into lockdown, Gareth wrote; "When we play again as an England team, it will be at a time when not only our country but the rest of the world as well is on the road to recovery. Hopefully we will be closer to each other than ever, and ready for the beautiful distraction that football can bring."

MEN'S SENIOR TEAM STAFF

Gareth Southgate is ably assisted in his role as England manager by the following individuals...

STEVE HOLLAND
Assistant Manager

An injury forced Steve Holland to retire from playing at the age of 21 following stints with Derby County, Bury, Husqvarna FF and Northwich Victoria. He was appointed as a youth coach at Crewe Alexandra in 1992 – aged just 22 at the time – having successfully completed the FA Full Coaching Licence. The Stockport-born coach eventually became Crewe's Academy Director while he jointly-managed first-team affairs at Gresty Road alongside Dario Gradi between July 2007 and November 2008.

Steve became Chelsea reserve team manager in 2009 before taking up a role of assistant first-team coach with the Blues in June 2011. He served under managers such as André Villas-Boas, Roberto Di Matteo, Rafael Benítez, José Mourinho, Gus Hiddink and Antonio Conte, during which time the West Londoners won the Premier League in both 2015 and 2017, the UEFA Champions League and FA Cup in 2012, the UEFA Europa League in 2013 and as well as the EFL Cup in 2015.

Steve's association with The FA began in 2013, as he worked alongside Gareth Southgate as England U21s assistant manager. He joined the senior Three Lions set-up on an interim basis in 2016 before leaving Chelsea at the end of the 2016/17 season to take up the role of England Men's Senior assistant manager full-time.

MARTYN MARGETSON
Goalkeeping Coach

Former Welsh international Martyn Margetson joined the England Senior Men's team as a goalkeeping coach in August 2016. The ex-Manchester City, Southend United, Huddersfield Town and Cardiff City player previously held a similar role with the Bluebirds as well as the Wales national team, Crystal Palace and Everton. In addition to his current responsibilities with England, Martyn is also a goalkeeping coach at Swansea City.

ALLAN RUSSELL
Attacking Coach

Allan Russell joined the England coaching staff in March 2017, with a focus on the attacking elements of the Three Lions' play. The Glasgow-born former striker started his playing career at Hibernian and after further spells in Scotland and England, turned out for Carolina RailHawks and Orange County Blues FC in the US, eventually retiring in 2014. Allan was praised by manager Gareth Southgate during the 2018 FIFA World Cup for his work on the Three Lions' set-pieces; nine of the 12 goals scored by the team at the tournament came from penalties, free-kicks and corners.

ENGLAND MEN'S SENIOR TEAM

NICKNAME:
The Three Lions

HEAD COACH:
Gareth Southgate

FIRST INTERNATIONAL:
Scotland 0-0 England,
30 November 1872

RECORD WIN:
England 13-0 Ireland,
31 July 1882

MOST CAPPED PLAYER:
Peter Shilton (125 caps)

RECORD GOAL-SCORER:
Wayne Rooney
(53 goals in 120 appearances)

TOURNAMENT RECORDS

FIFA WORLD CUP
Appearances at Tournament Finals: 15
Best Performance:
Winners 1966

UEFA EUROPEAN CHAMPIONSHIPS
Appearances at Tournament Finals: 10
(UEFA Euro 2020 will be England's 11th appearance at a European Championships Finals)
Best Performance:
Third place 1968 and 1996

UEFA NATIONS LEAGUE FINALS
Appearances at Tournament Finals: 1
Best Performance:
Third place 2019

(All information correct as of August 2019)

Gareth Southgate

Peter Shilton

Wayne Rooney

World Cup '66

SQUAD

GOALKEEPERS
JORDAN PICKFORD
JACK BUTLAND
TOM HEATON
NICK POPE
DEAN HENDERSON

DEFENDERS
KYLE WALKER
JOHN STONES
DANNY ROSE
HARRY MAGUIRE
MICHAEL KEANE
BEN CHILWELL
JOE GOMEZ
TRENT ALEXANDER-ARNOLD
KIERAN TRIPPIER
TYRONE MINGS
FIKAYO TOMORI

MIDFIELDERS
JORDAN HENDERSON
DELE
ROSS BARKLEY
JESSE LINGARD
FABIAN DELPH
DECLAN RICE
ALEX OXLADE-CHAMBERLAIN
MASON MOUNT
HARRY WINKS
JAMES MADDISON

FORWARDS
HARRY KANE
MARCUS RASHFORD
RAHEEM STERLING
JADON SANCHO
TAMMY ABRAHAM
CALLUM WILSON
CALLUM HUDSON-ODOI

(H) Home (A) Away (N) Neutral Venue

JORDAN PICKFORD

GOALKEEPER

Position: Goalkeeper **Date of Birth:** 07 March 1994
Place of Birth: Washington **England Debut:** 10 November 2017 v Germany (H)

Jordan was Men's Senior team's number one at the 2018 FIFA World Cup and excelled in the round of 16 clash against Colombia. After the match finished in a 1-1 draw after extra-time, the Everton stopper made a one-handed stop from a Carlos Bacca spot-kick to help the Three Lions to their first-ever World Cup penalty shootout success. He became the first English goalkeeper to take (and score) a penalty in a competitive shootout - and also made a save as England triumphed 6-5 on spot-kicks in the 2019 UEFA Nations League Finals third-place play-off against Switzerland in 2019.

JACK BUTLAND

GOALKEEPER

Position: Goalkeeper **Date of Birth:** 10 March 1993
Place of Birth: Bristol **England Debut:** 15 August 2012 v Italy (N)

Jack represented England at U16, U17, U19, U20 and U21 level and became the Men's Senior team's youngest-ever goalkeeper when he made his international debut at the age of 19 years and 158 days. His first competitive appearance for the Three Lions came in a 3-0 UEFA Euro 2016 qualifying victory in Lithuania in October 2015. Having suffered the disappointment of missing out on a place in Roy Hodgson's squad for UEFA Euro 2016 through injury, he made Gareth Southgate's 23-man squad for the FIFA World Cup two years later.

TOM HEATON

GOALKEEPER

Position: Goalkeeper **Date of Birth:** 15 April 1986
Place of Birth: Chester **England Debut:** 27 May 2016 v Australia (H)

Tom made his England debut as 87th-minute substitute for Fraser Forster against Australia at Sunderland AFC's Stadium of Light in May 2016 while he also featured in a friendly with Spain in November that year. The goalkeeper, who has been capped at U16, U17, U18, U19 and U21 level, made his first international start in a 3-2 away defeat to France in June 2017.

NICK POPE

GOALKEEPER

Position: Goalkeeper **Date of Birth:** 19 April 1992
Place of Birth: Soham **England Debut:** 06 June 2018 v Costa Rica (H)

Nick joined newly-promoted Premier League side Burnley in 2016 after a career that had previously seen him play in all three divisions of the EFL as well as the National League Premier Division, National League South and Isthmian League. The Clarets goalkeeper was part of the Three Lions' squad for the 2018 FIFA World Cup. His competitive debut came against Kosovo in a UEFA Euro 2020 qualifier in November 2019.

DEAN HENDERSON

GOALKEEPER

Position: Goalkeeper **Date of Birth:** 12 March 1997
Place of Birth: Whitehaven **England Debut:** -

Dean received his first call-up to the England Men's Senior squad in October 2019 after impressing in the Premier League whilst on loan from Manchester United to Sheffield United. The Cumbrian-born goalkeeper has been capped by England at U16, U17, U20 and U21 level and spent previous loan spells at Stockport County, Grimsby Town and Shrewsbury Town. He made 46 EFL Championship appearances for the Blades in 2018/19 as they were promoted to the top-flight.

KYLE WALKER

DEFENDER

Position: Defender **Date of Birth:** 28 May 1990

Place of Birth: Sheffield **England Debut:** 12 November 2011 v Spain (H)

A long-standing member of the England squad, Kyle was a few caps short of his 50th senior international appearance at the end of the 2019/20 season. Operating predominantly as a right-back during his career, Gareth Southgate opted to play the former Sheffield United and Tottenham Hotspur man as a centre-back at the 2018 FIFA World Cup. He previously featured for England at UEFA Euro 2016.

JOHN STONES

DEFENDER

Position: Defender **Date of Birth:** 28 May 1994

Place of Birth: Barnsley **England Debut:** 30 May 2014 v Peru (H)

John played in all seven of England's matches at the 2018 FIFA World Cup and scored twice in a 6-1 win over Panama at the tournament. He was also included in the Three Lions' squad for UEFA Euro 2016 and the 2019 UEFA Nations League finals. The two-time Premier League winner has previously been capped at U19, U20 and U21 level.

DANNY ROSE

DEFENDER

Position: Defender **Date of Birth:** 02 July 1990

Place of Birth: Doncaster **England Debut:** 26 March 2016 v Germany (A)

Prior to making his Three Lions debut in a memorable 3-2 win over Germany at the Olympiastadion in Berlin in March 2016, Danny was included in Great Britain's squad for the 2012 Olympic Games men's football tournament. The full-back had also been capped by England at U16, U17, U18 and U19 level while he won 29 caps for the U21s between 2009 and 2013, scoring three times. Danny has since played nearly 30 times for the Men's Senior team, featuring at both UEFA Euro 2016 and the 2018 FIFA World Cup.

HARRY MAGUIRE

DEFENDER

Position: Defender **Date of Birth:** 05 March 1993

Place of Birth: Sheffield **England Debut:** 08 October 2017 v Lithuania (A)

One of a number of Yorkshire-born defenders in Gareth Southgate's squad, Harry was part of an England defence that kept clean sheets in his first five senior international appearances against Lithuania, Germany, Brazil, Netherlands and Costa Rica. A year on from his memorable performances for the Three Lions at the 2018 FIFA World Cup – in which he featured in all seven games – the centre-back moved from Leicester City to Manchester United. He has won over 25 international caps since his England debut against Lithuania in 2017.

MICHAEL KEANE

DEFENDER

Position: Defender **Date of Birth:** 11 January 1993

Place of Birth: Stockport **England Debut:** 22 March 2017 v Germany (A)

After appearances for the Republic of Ireland's U17 and U19 teams, Michael switched his international allegiance to England in 2012 and was subsequently capped at U19, U20 and U21 level. His senior debut for the Three Lions came in in a 1-0 defeat to Germany in Dortmund in March 2017, while he also played in the 2-0 win over Lithuania at Wembley Stadium that same month. His first international goal came in an impressive 5-1 win away in Montenegro in a UEFA Euro 2020 qualifying match in March 2019.

BEN CHILWELL

DEFENDER

Position: Defender **Date of Birth:** 21 December 1996

Place of Birth: Milton Keynes **England debut:** 11 September 2018 v Switzerland (H)

Chelsea defender Ben made his senior England debut at his then-home club ground – the King Power Stadium – as the Three Lions beat Switzerland 1-0 in a friendly in September 2018. He made five appearances for England in 2018 and followed that up by winning six further caps in 2019, which included a start in the Three Lions' UEFA Nations League finals clash against the Netherlands in June 2019.

JOE GOMEZ

DEFENDER

Position: Defender **Date of Birth:** 23 May 1997

Place of Birth: London **England Debut:** 10 November 2017 v Germany (H)

Since moving to Liverpool from Charlton Athletic in 2015, Joe has won both the UEFA Champions League and Premier League title with the Reds. The former England U16, U17, U19 and U21 defender was named 'Man of the Match' in just his second Three Lions appearance as he helped nullify the attacking threat from the likes of Neymar, Gabriel Jesus and Philippe Coutinho in a goalless draw with Brazil in November 2017.

TRENT ALEXANDER-ARNOLD

DEFENDER

Position: Defender **Date of Birth:** 07 October 1998

Place of Birth: Liverpool **England Debut:** 07 June 2018 v Costa Rica (H)

By the time of his 22nd birthday, Trent had already made over 100 appearances for Liverpool in all competitions and won both the UEFA Champions League and Premier League with the Reds. The 2019 Ballon d'Or nominee had also established himself as a regular in the England Men's Senior squad, having made his Three Lions debut against Costa Rica in a friendly at Leeds United's Elland Road ground in June 2018. The right-back, who was part of England's 2018 FIFA World Cup squad, scored his first international goal in the 3-0 victory over the United States in November 2018.

KIERAN TRIPPIER

DEFENDER

Position: Defender **Date of Birth:** 19 September 1990

Place of Birth: Bury **England Debut:** 12 June 2017 v France (A)

Kieran provided England with one of the most memorable moments of the 2018 FIFA World Cup as his perfectly executed free-kick gave the Three Lions the lead in their semi-final clash with Croatia. He was ranked at the most creative player at the tournament, having created 24 chances in the six matches in which he featured. The Bury-born defender moved from Tottenham Hotspur to Atletico Madrid in the summer of 2019.

TYRONE MINGS

DEFENDER

Position: Defender **Date of Birth:** 13 March 1993

Place of Birth: Bath **England Debut:** 13 October 2019 v Bulgaria (A)

Tyrone completed his journey from non-League to international football in October 2019, when he made his Three Lions debut in a 6-0 away win in Bulgaria in a UEFA Euro 2020 qualifier. The defender's senior career started with the likes of Yate Town and Chippenham Town prior to a transfer to Ipswich Town in 2012. He has since played Premier League football for AFC Bournemouth and Aston Villa.

FIKAYO TOMORI

DEFENDER

Position: Defender **Date of Birth:** 19 December 1997

Place of Birth: Calgary, Canada **England Debut:** 17 November 2019 v Kosovo (A)

Fikayo Tomori was born in Canada to Nigerian parents and moved to England as a toddler. He started playing for Chelsea's U8s in 2005 and progressed through the ranks at the London club to make his senior debut for the Blues against Leicester City in May 2016. Loan spells at Brighton & Hove Albion, Hull City and Derby County followed before the defender returned to Chelsea, for whom he scored twice in 22 matches in 2019/20. The player, whose full name is Oluwafikayomi Oluwadamilola Tomori, turned out for Canada's U20s prior to committing his international allegiance to England, who whom he has been capped at U19, U20, U21 and senior level.

JORDAN HENDERSON

MIDFIELDER

Position: Midfielder **Date of Birth:** 17 June 1990

Place of Birth: Sunderland **England Debut:** 17 November 2010 v France (H)

A former captain of England's U21s, Jordan has won over 50 caps for the Men's Senior team since making his Three Lions debut against France at Wembley Stadium back in November 2010. The midfielder represented his country at the 2014 and 2018 FIFA World Cups as well as UEFA Euro 2012 and 2016 while he also played in the semi-final against the Netherlands at the 2019 UEFA National League finals. Jordan was named BT England Men's Senior Player of the Year in 2019.

DELE

MIDFIELDER

Position: Midfielder **Date of Birth:** 11 April 1996

Place of Birth: Milton Keynes **England Debut:** 09 October 2015 v Estonia (H)

Dele appeared for England at U17, U18, U19 and U21 level before making his senior debut for the Three Lions against Estonia in October 2015. The midfielder scored his first international in a 2-0 win over France at Wembley Stadium the following month. The two-time PFA Young Player of the Year was included in Gareth Southgate's squad for the 2018 FIFA World Cup, where he netted one goal in a 2-0 quarter-final victory against Sweden. Dele also featured in both of England's fixtures at the 2019 UEFA Nations League finals.

ROSS BARKLEY

MIDFIELDER

Position: Midfielder **Date of Birth:** 05 December 1993

Place of Birth: Liverpool **England Debut:** 06 September 2013 v Moldova (H)

Ross was part of England's victorious U17s squad that won the 2010 UEFA U17 Championships. Having also appeared at U16, U19, U20 and U21 level, the midfielder made his senior debut for the Three Lions in a 4-0 victory over Moldova at Wembley Stadium in September 2013. As of August 2020, the player had netted six times in 33 appearances for England.

JESSE LINGARD

MIDFIELDER

Position: Midfielder **Date of Birth:** 15 December 1992

Place of Birth: Warrington **England Debut:** 08 October 2016 v Malta (H)

Jesse made his England debut in Gareth Southgate's first match in charge of the national team – a 2-0 victory against Malta in October 2016. The pair had previously worked together at U21 level, with ten of Lingard's eleven caps for the Young Lions coming under Gareth's management. The attacking-midfielder has scored a number of notable goals in an England shirt, including a strike in the 6-1 triumph over Panama at the 2018 FIFA World Cup and the equaliser in a 2-1 triumph over Croatia in November 2018 which saw the Three Lions qualify for the UEFA Nations League finals.

FABIAN DELPH

MIDFIELDER

Position: Midfielder **Date of Birth:** 21 November 1989

Place of Birth: Bradford **England Debut:** 03 September 2014 v Norway (H)

A versatile player who can operate at left-back or across the midfield, Fabian featured in four matches for England at the 2018 FIFA World Cup. The former U19s and U21s international had the honour of captaining England in their 3-0 victory over the United States in November 2018 in the Wayne Rooney Foundation International. He passed the armband to Rooney, who came on as a 58th minute substitute for Jesse Lingard.

DECLAN RICE

MIDFIELDER

Position: Midfielder **Date of Birth:** 14 January 1999

Place of Birth: Kingston-upon-Thames **England Debut:** 22 March 2019 v Czech Republic (H)

After switching his international allegiance from the Republic of Ireland to England in February 2019, Declan made his Three Lions debut against Czech Republic the following month. He made a total of seven appearances for Gareth Southgate's team that year and played 105 minutes of the semi-final clash against the Netherlands – which saw the Dutch triumph 3-1 after extra-time - at the UEFA Nations League finals.

ALEX OXLADE-CHAMBERLAIN

MIDFIELDER

Position: Midfielder **Date of Birth:** 15 August 1993

Place of Birth: Portsmouth **England Debut:** 26 May 2012 v Norway (A)

Son of the former England international Mark Chamberlain, Alex has won over 30 caps for the Three Lions. The 'Ox' played in three of England's matches at UEFA Euro 2012 and was included in the squad for the 2014 FIFA World Cup. His first senior international goal came against San Marino in October 2012 and he came on as a second-half substitute to score in an away friendly against Brazil in June 2013 which marked the opening of the refurbished Maracana Stadium.

MASON MOUNT

MIDFIELDER

Position: Midfielder **Date of Birth:** 10 January 1999

Place of Birth: Portsmouth **England Debut:** 06 September 2019 v Bulgaria (H)

Mason was the named 'Golden Player' (player of the tournament) at the 2017 UEFA European U19 Championships, which saw the Young Lions triumph in Georgia. In addition to the U19s, the midfielder also appeared at U16, U17, U18 and U21 level. A product of Chelsea's youth academy, Mason featured in six matches in qualifying for UEFA Euro 2020 and scored his first goal for the team in a 4-0 away win in Kosovo.

HARRY WINKS

MIDFIELDER

Position: Midfielder **Date of Birth:** 02 February 1996

Place of Birth: Hemel Hempstead **England Debut:** 07 October 2017 v Lithuania (A)

Like England captain Harry Kane, midfielder Harry Winks progressed through the academy system at Tottenham Hotspur. Harry made his senior club debut in 2014 while his first appearance for England followed three years later as he started in a 1-0 win over Lithuania in a 2018 FIFA World Cup qualifier. He missed the 2018 FIFA World Cup due to injury but featured in the 2018/19 UEFA Nations League campaign, which included an appearance in the 3-2 win in Spain. His first international goal came against Kosovo in November 2019.

JAMES MADDISON

MIDFIELDER

Position: Midfielder **Date of Birth:** 23 November 1996

Place of Birth: Coventry **England Debut:** 14 November 2019 v Montenegro (H)

After some fine performances for Leicester City, James was originally called up to the Senior Men's squad for matches against Croatia and Spain in 2018 although he had to wait over a year before making his England debut. The midfielder started his career with the likes of Coventry City, Norwich City and Aberdeen (loan) before moving to the King Power Stadium in 2018. He has nine England U21s caps to his name and was included in the 23-man squad for the 2019 UEFA European U21 Championship.

HARRY KANE

FORWARD

Position: Forward **Date of Birth:** 28 July 1993

Place of Birth: London **England Debut:** 27 March 2015 v Lithuania (H)

Harry made an instant impact in an England shirt, netting after just 80 seconds of his senior international debut against Lithuania in March 2015 having come on as a substitute for Wayne Rooney. The forward has continued in a rich vein of goal scoring form for the Three Lions ever since. He won the Golden Boot award at the 2018 FIFA World Cup with six strikes in as many games while he was the top goal scorer in UEFA Euro 2020 qualifying with 12 goals in eight matches. He bagged a hat-trick in the 7-0 win over Montenegro in November 2019 that confirmed England's place at the finals of the European Championship.

MARCUS RASHFORD

FORWARD

Position: Forward **Date of Birth:** 31 October 1997

Place of Birth: Manchester **England Debut:** 27 May 2016 v Australia (H)

At the age of 18 years and 208 days, Marcus became the youngest player ever to score on his England debut, netting in the Three Lions' 2-1 victory over Australia at Sunderland AFC's Stadium of Light in May 2016. The forward, who previously represented the Young Lions at U16, U18, U20 and U21 level, scored three goals in qualification for UEFA Euro 2020 with strikes against Bulgaria (away), Montenegro (home) and Kosovo (away).

RAHEEM STERLING

FORWARD

Position: Forward **Date of Birth:** 08 December 1994

Place of Birth: Kingston, Jamaica **England Debut:** 14 November 2012 v Sweden (A)

In November 2012, Raheem became the fifth-youngest player ever to debut for England at the age of just 17 years and 332 days as he started in a 4-2 away defeat to Sweden. The Manchester City forward has since made over 50 appearances for the Three Lions and was included in the squad for the 2014 and 2018 FIFA World Cups, UEFA Euro 2016 and the UEFA Nations League finals in 2019. Raheem's first international goal came in a 4-0 victory over Lithuania in March 2015, while he bagged a memorable brace in a 3-2 away win in Spain in October 2018. His first international hat-trick meanwhile came in the 5-0 demolition of Czech Republic in March 2019.

JADON SANCHO

FORWARD

Position: Forward **Date of Birth:** 25 March 2000

Place of Birth: London **England Debut:** 12 October 2018 v Croatia (A)

Jadon was part of the Young Lions squad that won the FIFA U17 World Cup in India back in 2017. The forward scored 14 goals in 18 appearances for the U17s between 2016 and 2017 and is also capped at U16s and U19s level. His first international goals came as he bagged a brace in a 5-3 victory over Kosovo at Southampton's St Mary's Stadium in September 2019.

TAMMY ABRAHAM

FORWARD

Position: Forward **Date of Birth:** 02 October 1997

Place of Birth: London **England Debut:** 10 November 2017 v Germany (H)

Tammy won his first England caps as the Three Lions hosted Germany and Brazil in friendly matches in November 2017. His first competitive appearance came in a 2-1 away defeat to Czech Republic in October 2019 in a UEFA Euro 2020 qualifier while his first international goal came in a 7-0 victory over Montenegro the following month. The Chelsea forward has previously been capped at U18, U19 and U21 level.

CALLUM WILSON

FORWARD

Position: Forward **Date of Birth:** 27 February 1992

Place of Birth: Coventry **England Debut:** 15 November 2018 v United States (H)

Callum made a strong start to his England career, scoring against the United States in November 2018 having previously been capped as an U21 player back in 2014. In 2019, the striker won three further caps for the Three Lions with appearances against Montenegro (away), Switzerland (neutral) and Bulgaria (away) after impressing Gareth Southgate with his performances for AFC Bournemouth.

CALLUM HUDSON-ODOI

FORWARD

Position: Forward **Date of Birth:** 07 November 2000

Place of Birth: London **England Debut:** 22 March 2019 v Czech Republic (H)

Callum made 22 appearances for England U17s between 2016 and 2017 as well as featuring for the Young Lions at U16, U18 and U19 level. He became the youngest-ever player to feature in a senior competitive match for England when he was introduced as a substitute in a 5-0 win over Czech Republic in March 2019 at the age of 18 years and 135 days. His U21s debut came in a 2-2 draw with Slovenia U21s in October 2019.

MEN'S SENIOR TEAM TOP TENS

TEN MOST CAPPED ENGLAND PLAYERS OF ALL TIME

	PLAYER	ENGLAND CAREER	CAPS	GOALS
1st	Peter Shilton	1970–1990	125	0
2nd	Wayne Rooney	2003–2018	120	53
3rd	David Beckham	1996–2009	115	17
4th	Steven Gerrard	2000–2014	114	21
5th	Bobby Moore	1962–1973	108	2
6th	Ashley Cole	2001–2014	107	0
Joint 7th	Bobby Charlton	1958–1970	106	49
Joint 7th	Frank Lampard	1999–2014	106	29
9th	Billy Wright	1946–1959	105	3
10th	Bryan Robson	1980–1991	90	26

TEN MOST PROLIFIC ENGLAND GOALSCORERS OF ALL TIME

	PLAYER	ENGLAND CAREER	CAPS	GOALS
1st	Wayne Rooney	2003–2018	120	53
2nd	Bobby Charlton	1958–1970	106	49
3rd	Gary Lineker	1984–1992	80	48
4th	Jimmy Greaves	1959–1967	57	44
5th	Michael Owen	1998–2008	89	40
6th	Harry Kane	2015–to date	45	32
Joint 7th	Nat Lofthouse	1950–1958	33	30
Joint 7th	Alan Shearer	1992–2000	63	30
Joint 7th	Tom Finney	1946–1958	76	30
Joint 10th	Vivian Woodward	1903–1911	73	29
Joint 10th	Frank Lampard	1999–2014	106	29

(All information correct as of August 2020)

PETER SHILTON

WAYNE ROONEY

DAVID BECKHAM

BOBBY CHARLTON

GARY LINEKER

UEFA EURO 2020 IN OPPOSITION

Prior to UEFA Euro 2020 kicking off in the summer of 2021, we take a look at England's Group D opponents at the tournament.

Managers: Gareth Southgate, Zlatko Dalic & Jaroslav Šilhavý

CROATIA

LOWDOWN

Since taking part in their first tournament in 1996, where they reached the quarter-finals, Croatia have qualified for all but one (UEFA Euro 2000) of the subsequent European Championships. The 2018 FIFA World Cup runners-up made it to the round of 16 stage at UEFA Euro 2016 while they achieved qualification to UEFA Euro 2020 by topping qualifying Group E. Bruno Petkovic was Croatia's top scorer in qualifying, with four goals.

Luka Modric

MANAGER

Croatia have been managed by **Zlatko Dalic** since 2017. As a result of their run to the World Cup Final in 2018, the 'Vatreni' (Blazers) rose to fourth place in the FIFA World Ranking ranking in August of that year.

STAR MAN

Luka Modric is likely to skipper Croatia at UEFA Euro 2020 in what will be his seventh major tournament with his country. The 2018 Ballon d'Or winner has collected over 125 caps since making his senior debut for the Vatreni against Argentina in Basel on 1 March 2006.

CZECH REPUBLIC

LOWDOWN

The Czech Republic secured qualification to UEFA Euro 2020 by finishing as runners-up to England in qualifying Group A. Jaroslav Silhavy's side won five of their eight qualifying fixtures and inflicted the Three Lions only defeat of the campaign in Prague in October 2019.

Harry Kane & Ondrej Celustka battle for the ball

The former Czechoslovakia were European champions in 1976 and finished third at the tournament in both 1960 and 1980. Following the split of Czechoslovakia into two sovereign states – the Czech Republic and Slovakia - in 1993, the Czech Republic have qualified for every European Championships since and made it to the semi-finals in 2004.

MANAGER

Former defender **Jaroslav Šilhavý** won four caps for Czechoslovakia between 1990 and 1991 and served as the Czech Republic's assistant manager between 2001 and 2009. He became manager of the Czech Republic in 2018 after spells in charge of club sides including Slovan Liberec, Jablonec, Dukla Prague and Slavia Prague.

STAR MAN

Patrik Schick scored four of the Czech Republic's 13 goals in qualifying, including a brace in a 2-1 victory over Bulgaria on 7 June 2019. The Prague-born forward spent the 2019/20 season on loan with Bundesliga giants RB Leipzig.

Patrik Schick

PLAY-OFF WINNER C

LOWDOWN

Due to the postponement of the UEFA Euro 2020 play-off matches originally scheduled for March 2020 (and subsequently June 2020), England's final Group D opponents were unknown at the time of writing. The winners of play-off path C will eventually take their place in the group with the two play-off semi-finals seeing Scotland take on Israel and Norway face Serbia.

Goal scorers Alan Shearer & Paul Gascoigne

In the event of Scotland's progression to the finals, memories would surely be rekindled of the UEFA Euro 1996 clash between the Tartan Army and the Three Lions at Wembley Stadium. England triumphed 2-0 on that occasion thanks to a strike from Alan Shearer and a wonder goal from Paul Gascoigne.
The 'auld enemies' have met 114 times to date, with the first official clash taking place back in November 1872.

England last faced Israel back in 2007 in two qualifying matches for UEFA Euro 2008 while their most recent encounter with Norway was a friendly at Wembley Stadium in September 2014. England are yet to play Serbia at senior international level.

Alex Oxlade-Chamberlain & Ruben Yttergard Jenssen

WEMBLEY CLASSICS

As Wembley Stadium gears up to stage seven games in this summer's UEFA Euro 2020 tournament, including the final of the competition, we take a look at some other major matches that have taken place at the venue since its opening back in 2007.

FIRST MATCH

England U21 3-3 Italy U21s
U21 Friendly International, 24 March 2007

David Bentley, Wayne Routledge and Matt Derbyshire all scored for England U21s in an entertaining clash with their Italian counterparts in March 2007. A sell-out crowd – albeit one restricted in size to 55,700 – saw the first-ever football match to be staged at the 'new' Wembley Stadium. Giampaolo Pazzini scored the venue's first hat-trick for the visitors.

BLUE IS THE COLOUR

Chelsea 1-0 Manchester United (after extra-time)
FA Cup Final, 19 May 2007

Didier Drogba loved playing at Wembley Stadium, scoring no less than eight goals in various competitions at the venue. His extra-time winner against Manchester United in 2007 saw Chelsea triumph in the first FA Cup Final to be played at the new stadium.

SEE YOU IN SOUTH AFRICA!

England 5-1 Croatia
2010 FIFA World Cup Qualifier
9 September 2009

After the heartbreak of missing out on qualification for UEFA Euro 2008, England bounced back with an emphatic performance to seal their place at the 2010 FIFA World Cup in South Africa. A penalty from Frank Lampard – the first of his two goals on the night – put the Three Lions one up after just eight minutes. A brace from fellow midfielder Steven Gerrard and a further strike from Wayne Rooney wrapped up the win for England while their Wembley visitors, Croatia, got a consolation through Eduardo.

MESSI-MASTERCLASS

Barcelona 3-1 Manchester United
UEFA Champions League Final
28 May 2011

Lionel Messi scored and was named 'Man of the Match' in Barcelona's 3-1 win over Manchester United in the 2011 UEFA Champions League Final. Pedro and David Villa were also on target for the La Liga giants while Wayne Rooney – England's record goal scorer with 53 strikes in 120 appearances – managed a Wembley strike for his then-club side, Manchester United.

GOLDEN MOMENT

Mexico 2-1 Brazil
2012 Olympic Games – Men's Football Gold Medal Match, 11 August 2012

Wembley Stadium hosted numerous football matches during the 2012 Olympic Games, including Great Britain men's 3-1 victory over the United Arab Emirates and Great Britain women's memorable 1-0 triumph over Brazil. The Gold Medal Match of both the men's and women's competitions were staged at Wembley too. The United States beat Japan 2-1 in the women's match while a brace from Oribe Peralta saw Mexico men's team triumph 2-1 against Brazil.

ALL-GERMAN AFFAIR

Bayern Munich 2-1 Borussia Dortmund
UEFA Champions League Final, 25 May 2013

Two years on from Barcelona's victory over Manchester United, the UEFA Champions League Final returned to Wembley Stadium in 2013. An all-German showdown between Borussia Dortmund and Bayern Munich ended in a 2-1 triumph for Bayern thanks to goals from Mario Mandzukic and Arjen Robben.

CUP FINAL FIRST

Chelsea Women 1-0 Notts County Women
FA Women's Cup Final
1 August 2015

The Women's FA Cup Final has been staged at Wembley Stadium since 2015. Chelsea Women beat Notts County 1-0 in the first of those finals thanks to a strike from South Korean international Ji So-Yun.

HOT-SPURS

Tottenham Hotspur 3-1 Real Madrid
UEFA Champions League
1 November 2017

Tottenham Hotspur temporarily played their home matches in the UEFA Champions League at Wembley Stadium between September 2016 and February 2019, while they also staged their Premier League matches there between August 2017 and March 2019. Perhaps Spurs' finest win at their temporary home was a 3-1 triumph over then-holders Real Madrid in November 2017.

ALL IN ATTENDENCE

England Women 1-2 Germany Women
Women's International Friendly, 9 November 2019

Having previously attracted their record home crowd of 45,619 for a match against Germany in 2014, England's Senior Women's side returned to the 'Home of Football' in 2019 for another clash against the same opponents. A new record crowd figure of 77,768 was set that evening as Phil Neville's Lionesses went down to a 2-1 defeat.

SEVEN-UP

England 7-0 Montenegro
UEFA Euro 2020 Qualifying
14 November 2019

England secured qualification to UEFA Euro 2020 in style as a Harry Kane hat-trick helped the Three Lions beat Montenegro 7-0. Alex Oxlade-Chamberlain, Marcus Rashford and Tammy Abraham also scored in the Three Lions' 1,000th Men's Senior international match while Aleksandar Sofranac put through his own net.

LIONESSES IN LOCKDOWN

Just days after England Senior Women's team played their final match at the 2020 SheBelieves Cup (a 1-0 defeat to Spain on 11 March 2020), football activity in the United Kingdom was suspended as a result of the COVID-19 pandemic. With the 2019/20 Barclays FA WSL season (and many other leagues around the world) having to be cancelled and Lionesses matches put on hold, we take a look back at what England's players got up to during a challenging period...

LIONESSES COFFEE CLUB

Jill Scott **Karen Bardsley**

As the nation went into lockdown, the Lionesses came up with a novel way of keeping in touch with one another - as well as their fans - by launching the 'Lionesses Coffee Club'. Each week Jill Scott and Karen Bardsley spoke with two of their England colleagues , with Carly Telford and Jodie Taylor the show's first guests.

As Karen explained. "The Lionesses Coffee Club is just a way for us all to keep in touch with each other while we're all in social isolation. This [meeting for coffee] was something we used to like to do so often when we were together. Obviously, we can't [meet during lockdown] and it's a nice way for all of us to check in on each other and see how we're getting on through Google Meet. We hope it's a fun way to keep in touch and bring a little entertainment to everyone's day."

"I think it's a really good idea because we go for coffee on camp all the time, so [though] we're not on camp together we're still having coffee and anyone who's a fan or likes to watch the Lionesses can grab one as well and feel like they're having a coffee with us," added Carly.

Rachel Daly **Millie Bright**

Along with Rachel Daly, Millie Bright was a guest on Episode 3 of the Coffee Club and she took the opportunity to pay tribute to her sister and aunt, who had key frontline roles in the midst of the pandemic. Millie's aunt was the Chief Operating Officer at one of the Nightingale Hospitals - which were created in response to COVID-19 - while her sister is a staff nurse. She ended her appearance on the show by saying: "I'd like to dedicate this one to my auntie and my sister, working on the front line, day in and day out."

PHONE A KEY WORKER

Millie was amongst a host of Lionesses who called a key worker during lockdown and thanked them for their tireless efforts during such challenging times. She got in touch with primary school teacher Sophie Read on 'Thank a Teacher Day' while Ellen White checked in with Kristen Whitfield – a nursing assistant from Tyne and Wear who worked for the Sunderland GP Alliance during the pandemic. Lucy Bronze surprised supermarket team leader Michelle France while another touching conversation saw Nikita Parris congratulate Gemma Batey of Ouston Junior Girls U14s for becoming the one millionth grassroots player to register with The FA's Whole Game System.

#FOOTBALLSSTAYINGHOME

The likes of Lucy Bronze, Alex Greenwood, Georgia Stanway and Jordan Nobbs linked up with Google Cloud to back a campaign to 'kick Coronavirus', urging people across the UK to stay home, protect the NHS and save lives during the lockdown period. Lionesses captain Steph Houghton joined Three Lions skipper Harry Kane meanwhile to launch #FootballsStayingHome – a campaign across The FA's channels which was designed to inform, entertain and empower millions of England fans.

Content across various channels aimed to keep spirits up and keep people active both physically and mentally. Features of #FootballsStayingHome included motivational advice, throwbacks to classic England matches and virtual 'skill schools'. Jill Scott hosted 'Obvious Jill's Football Skills', which saw the midfielder try out some of her Lionesses teammates' signature moves, such as Keira Walsh's 'snake hips', which has helped the Manchester City player escape defenders when representing both her club and country!

Steph Houghton

Harry Kane

LOOKING AHEAD TO 2022

The postponement of UEFA Euro 2020 until the summer of 2021 also meant UEFA were forced to move UEFA Women's EURO from 2021 to 2022.

The 16-team tournament will now be staged in England between 6 and 31 July 2022. The Lionesses will feature in the first match of the competition at Old Trafford, Manchester on 6 July 2022 while they will play their other Group A fixtures at the Brighton Community Stadium and St Mary's Stadium in Southampton.

Commenting on the decision to move the tournament from 2021 to 2022, UEFA's chief of women's football Nadine Kessler commented;

"We firmly believe that this decision is in the best interests of the tournament, the players, the fans, women's football partners and everybody involved in all areas and at all levels of the game. UEFA Women's EURO is Europe's biggest women's sport event, as well as a major event in worldwide terms. For this reason alone, it's deserving of its own special and privileged platform."

Sue Campbell, The FA's Director of Women's Football added;

"Moving the tournament to 2022, coupled with the postponement of the Olympics until 2021, does of course mean the Lionesses won't have a major tournament for longer than expected or planned for.

"While unexpected, the move will also present both our Lionesses and their fans with an exciting roadmap for the next few years – with Team GB representation at the Olympic Games in 2021, a home EURO in 2022 and a FIFA World Cup in 2023. I'm confident that it will be worth the wait!"

ENGLAND WOMEN'S SENIOR TEAM

NICKNAME:
The Lionesses

HEAD COACH:
Phil Neville (until July 2021) / Sarina Wiegman (from September 2021)

FIRST INTERNATIONAL:
Scotland 2-3 England, 18 November 1972

RECORD WIN:
Hungary 0-13 England, 27 October 2005

MOST CAPPED PLAYER:
Fara Williams (170 caps)

RECORD GOAL-SCORER:
Kelly Smith (46 goals in 117 appearances)

TOURNAMENT RECORDS

FIFA WOMEN'S WORLD CUP
Appearances at Tournament Finals: 5
Best Performance: Third place, 2015

UEFA WOMEN'S CHAMPIONSHIPS
Appearances at Tournament Finals: 8 (UEFA Women's Euro 2021 – to be staged in 2022 - will be England's ninth appearance at a UEFA Women's Championships Finals)
Best Performance:
Runners-up 1984 and 2009

SHEBELIEVES CUP
Appearances at Tournament Finals: 5
Best Performance: Winners in 2019

(All information correct as of August 2020)

Phil Neville

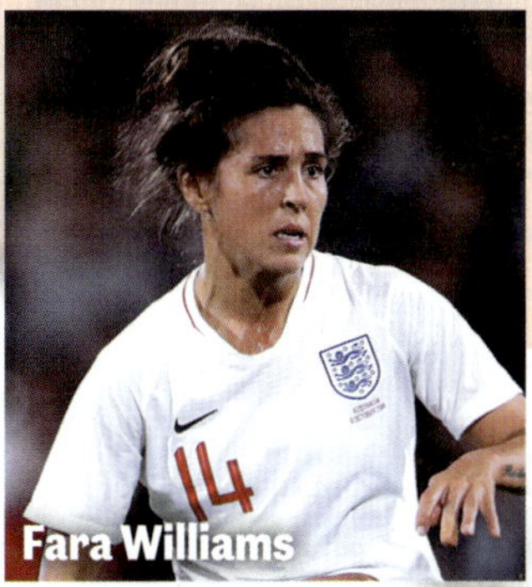
Fara Williams

Kelly Smith

She Believes Cup 2019

SQUAD

GOALKEEPERS
KAREN BARDSLEY
CARLY TELFORD
ELLIE ROEBUCK
MARY EARPS

DEFENDERS
LUCY BRONZE
MILLIE BRIGHT
RACHEL DALY
ALEX GREENWOOD
STEPH HOUGHTON
ABBIE McMANUS
DEMI STOKES
LEAH WILLIAMSON

MIDFIELDERS
JORDAN NOBBS
JILL SCOTT
LUCY STANIFORTH
GEORGIA STANWAY
KEIRA WALSH
JADE MOORE
MELISSA LAWLEY

FORWARDS
ELLEN WHITE
TONI DUGGAN
BETHANY ENGLAND
LAUREN HEMP
CHLOE KELLY
NIKITA PARRIS
BETH MEAD
FRAN KIRBY
JODIE TAYLOR

(H) Home (A) Away (N) Neutral Venue

KAREN BARDSLEY

GOALKEEPER

Position: Goalkeeper **Date of Birth:** 14 October 1984
Place of Birth: Santa Monica, United States
England Debut: 09 March 2005 v Northern Ireland (N)

Born in the United States to English parents, Karen has been a regular starter for England since making her Lionesses' debut in the 2005 Algarve Cup. The 5ft 11" stopper has won over 80 caps for the Women's Senior team to date and was included in the squad for the 2011, 2015 and 2019 FIFA Women's World Cups. She was also part of the England 22 that finished as runners-up at the 2009 UEFA Women's European Championships and travelled with the Lionesses to the 2013 and 2017 tournaments.

CARLY TELFORD

GOALKEEPER

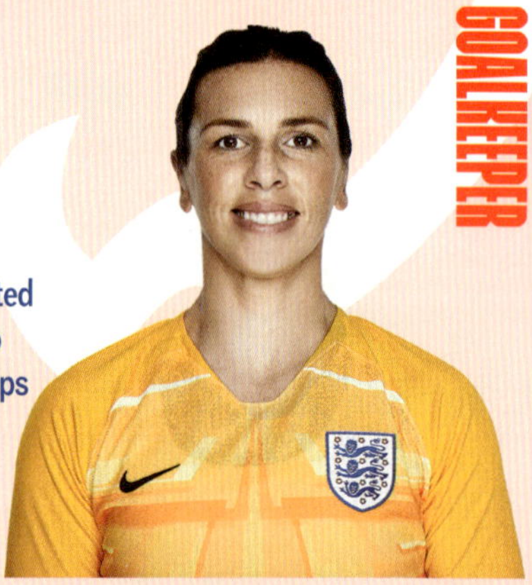

Position: Goalkeeper **Date of Birth:** 07 July 1987
Place of Birth: Newcastle **England Debut:** 11 March 2007 v Scotland (H)

Just six months after making her senior debut for England, Carly was part of the Lionesses' squad for the 2007 FIFA Women's World Cup. Having previously represented England at U17, U19, U21 and U23 level, the goalkeeper has won over 20 senior caps to date. Having been an unused substitute at the 2007 and 2015 FIFA Women's World Cups as well as UEFA Women's Euro 2017, Carly made three appearances at the 2019 FIFA World Cup. She also started in two matches at the 2020 SheBelieves Cup.

ELLIE ROEBUCK

GOALKEEPER

Position: Goalkeeper **Date of Birth:** 23 September 1999
Place of Birth: Sheffield **England Debut:** 08 November 2018 v Austria (A)

A product of Sheffield United's Centre of Excellence, Ellie was part of the Young Lionesses squad that finished third at the 2018 FIFA U20 Women's World Cup prior to making her senior England debut later that year. The 5ft 8" Manchester City stopper was included in the squad for the 2020 SheBelieves Cup, which saw her keep a clean sheet in the 1-0 win over Japan at the Red Bull Arena in Harrison, New Jersey.

MARY EARPS

GOALKEEPER

Position: Goalkeeper **Date of Birth:** 07 March 1993
Place of Birth: Nottingham **England Debut:** 10 June 2017 v Switzerland (A)

During her time at Loughborough University, Mary was part of the same Great Britain squad as Isobel Christiansen, Fran Kirby, Kerys Harrop and Demi Stokes that won gold at the 2013 World University Games. Having represented England at U17, U19 and U23 level, the goalkeeper received her first Lionesses' call-up for a match against Montenegro in April 2014 but had to wait over three years to make her senior debut. A member of Phil Neville's squads for the SheBelieves Cup and the FIFA Women's World Cup in 2019, Mary moved from VfL Wolfsburg to Manchester United that same year.

LUCY BRONZE

DEFENDER

Position: Defender **Date of Birth:** 28 October 1991
Place of Birth: Berwick-upon-Tweed **England Debut:** 26 June 2013 v Japan (H)

Lucy became the first English footballer to be named as the UEFA Women's Player of the Year Award in 2019 after a year that saw her win four major trophies with her club side, Olympique Lyonnais. She also picked up the BT England Women's Senior Player of the Year award (see pages 44 and 45) in January 2020 after appearing in 18 of England's 20 fixtures during the previous year as the Lionesses reached the FIFA Women's World Cup semi-finals – where she collected the Silver Ball award - and won the SheBelievesCup.

MILLIE BRIGHT

DEFENDER

Position: Defender **Date of Birth:** 21 August 1993
Place of Birth: Chesterfield **England Debut:** 19 September 2016 v Belgium (A)

After the disappointment of missing out on the 2019 SheBelieves Cup triumph through injury, Millie was an ever-present at the 2020 tournament, starting matches against the United States, Japan and Spain. The defender also featured in five of the Lionesses' seven matches at the 2019 FIFA Women's World Cup. The former England U19 and U23 international, who was selected in all of the Lionesses' matches at UEFA Women's Euro 2017, had won 37 caps for the Lionesses at the time of writing.

RACHEL DALY

DEFENDER

Position: Defender/Forward **Date of Birth:** 06 December 1991
Place of Birth: Harrogate **England Debut:** 03 June 2016 v Serbia (H)

Rachel scored during her England debut in a 7-0 victory over Serbia in a UEFA Women's Euro 2017 qualifier. Since then, the versatile player – who can operate in defence or attack – has won over 35 caps for the Lionesses and was named in the squad for the 2019 FIFA Women's World Cup as well as the squads for the 2018, 2019 and 2020 SheBelieves Cups. The former Leeds United youth player has been capped at U15, U16, U19 and U23 level.

ALEX GREENWOOD

DEFENDER

Position: Defender **Date of Birth:** 07 September 1993
Place of Birth: Liverpool **England Debut:** 05 March 2014 v Italy (N)

Alex was one of England's stars of the 2019 FIFA Women's World Cup, which saw her feature in four matches and score a memorable goal against Cameroon in the round of 16. At the age of 22, Alex was thc youngest member of the Lionesses' squad which finished third at the 2015 FIFA Women's World Cup. She started in the third-place play-off win over Germany at that tournament, and was a key member of the squad that reached the semi-finals of UEFA Women's Euro 2017.

STEPH HOUGHTON

DEFENDER

Position: Defender **Date of Birth:** 23 April 1988
Place of Birth: Durham **England Debut:** 08 March 2007 v Russia (H)

Steph is the Lionesses' long-serving captain, with over 100 caps to her name. She missed the 2007 FIFA Women's World Cup and UEFA Women's Euro 2009 through injury but has featured at every major tournament since. She captained England to third and fourth place finishes at the 2015 and 2019 FIFA Women's World Cups respectively, as well as skippering the side which reached the semi-finals of UEFA Women's Euro 2017. A superb ambassador for her sport, Steph launched The FA's 'Pledge of Positivity' with Men's Senior team captain Harry Kane in February 2020 (see pages 40 and 41) and was appointed a Member of the Order of the British Empire (MBE) back in 2016 for her services to football.

ABBIE McMANUS

DEFENDER

Position: Defender **Date of Birth:** 14 January 1993
Place of Birth: Prestwich **England Debut:** 01 March 2018 v France (N)

Abbie made three appearances – including two starts – for England at the 2019 FIFA Women's World Cup while she started in two of the Lionesses' matches at the SheBelieves Cup earlier in the year, which saw the Lionesses win the tournament. After a total of 12 years with Manchester City, the defender announced her departure to rivals Manchester United – the club she had supported as a youngster - in May 2019.

DEMI STOKES

DEFENDER

Position: Defender **Date of Birth:** 12 December 1991
Place of Birth: Dudley **England Debut:** 17 January 2014 v Norway (N)

Demi represented England at U19, U20 and U23 level prior to her inclusion in the senior squad for a training camp in La Manga, Spain in 2014 during which time she made her Lionesses debut in a 1-1 friendly draw with Norway. The defender has won over 50 caps to date, with her one international goal at the time of writing having come in a 9-0 victory over Montenegro in a 2015 FIFA Women's World Cup qualifier in Brighton in April 2014.

LEAH WILLIAMSON

DEFENDER

Position: Defender **Date of Birth:** 29 March 1997
Place of Birth: Milton Keynes **England Debut:** 08 June 2018 v Russia (A)

Leah has been a regular member of the Lionesses squad in recent years and appeared in all three of their matches at the 2020 SheBelieves Cup. Having featured for England at various youth and development stages between U15 and U23 level, the defender first appeared for the senior side as a substitute in a 3-1 victory in Russia in June 2018. She was named in Phil Neville's squad for the 2019 FIFA Women's World Cup, which saw her make her tournament debut as a substitute against Cameroon. A product of Arsenal's Centre of Excellence, the defender won her first Barclays FA WSL with the north Londoners in 2019.

JORDAN NOBBS

MIDFIELDER

Position: Midfielder **Date of Birth:** 08 December 1992
Place of Birth: Stockton-on-Tees **England Debut:** 06 March 2013 v Italy (N)

Jordan was called into the England U15 squad at the age of 12 and captained the side against Wales U15s when she was just 13. She was also capped at U17, U19, U20 and U23 prior to making her senior Lionesses debut four years on from being a key member of the squad that won the 2009 UEFA Women's U19 Championship. Having appeared for the Lionesses at the 2013 and 2017 UEFA Women's Championships and the 2015 FIFA Women's World Cup, the midfielder suffered the heartbreak of missing out on the 2019 FIFA Women's World Cup with a knee injury. She returned to the Lionesses' line-up for matches with Brazil and Portugal in October 2019 and appeared in all three games at the 2020 SheBelieves Cup.

JILL SCOTT

MIDFIELDER

Position: Midfielder **Date of Birth:** 02 February 1987
Place of Birth: Sunderland **England Debut:** 30 August 2006 v Netherlands (H)

As the United Kingdom went into lockdown in 2020 in the midst of the COVID-19 pandemic, Jill entertained countless Lionesses' fans by taking to social media and hosting the 'Lionesses Coffee Club' with teammate Karen Bardsley and presenting 'Obvious Jill's Football Skills'. Having played over 140 matches since making her debut in a 4-0 victory over the Netherlands in August 2006, Jill is one of just 11 Lionesses centurions. She has been selected in the squad for seven major tournaments to date – the FIFA Women's World Cup in 2007, 2011, 2015 and 2019 as well as the UEFA Women's European Championships in 2009, 2013 and 2017.

LUCY STANIFORTH

MIDFIELDER

Position: Midfielder **Date of Birth:** 02 October 1992
Place of Birth: York **England Debut:** 03 September 2018 v Kazakhstan (A)

Lucy helped England to victory at the 2019 SheBelieves Cup, scoring the opening goal in a 3-0 win over Japan at the tournament. She also appeared at the 2020 competition, coming on as a second-half substitute for Georgia Stanway in the 1-0 triumph over Japan. The midfielder, who signed for Manchester United in July 2020, has made over 15 appearances for England to date having previously featured at U17, U19, U20 and U23 level. She was included in the 23-player squad for the 2019 FIFA Women's World Cup.

GEORGIA STANWAY

MIDFIELDER

Position: Midfielder **Date of Birth:** 03 January 1999
Place of Birth: Barrow-in-Furness England Debut: 08 November 2018 v Austria (A)

On the back of being named the PFA Women's Young Player of the Year in 2018/19, Georgia was the youngest player to be included in Phil Neville's squad for the 2019 FIFA Women's World Cup. The then-20-year-old went on to feature in five matches at the tournament. Previously capped at U15, U17, U19 and U20 level, the midfielder was the joint top-goal scorer at the 2018 FIFA U20 World Cup in France with six strikes, as the Young Lionesses finished third at the tournament. Later that year, she scored on her England debut in a 3-0 win over Austria.

KEIRA WALSH

MIDFIELDER

Position: Midfielder **Date of Birth:** 08 April 1997
Place of Birth: Rochdale **England Debut:** 28 November 2017 v Kazakhstan (H)

One of England's main playmakers, Keira captained the Lionesses for the first time in a 6-0 win over Kazakhstan in September 2018 – less than 12 months on from making her senior international debut - aged just 21 at the time. The midfielder appeared in all three of England's matches at both the 2019 and 2020 SheBelieves Cup tournaments. She was included in the squad for the 2019 FIFA Women's World Cup where she featured in five matches.

JADE MOORE

MIDFIELDER

Position: Midfielder **Date of Birth:** 22 October 1990
Place of Birth: Worksop **England Debut:** 28 February 2012 v Finland (N)

A former U19, U20 and U23 international, Jade was included in the Lionesses' squad for the 2013 and 2017 UEFA Women's European Championships and the 2015 and 2019 FIFA Women's World Cups. She played in four matches at the latter tournament, with her start against Sweden in the third-place play-off marking her 50th senior appearance for England. At club level, the former Lincoln City, Leeds United, Birmingham City, Notts County and Reading player currently plies her trade for Orlando Pride in the National Women's Soccer League in the United States.

MELISSA LAWLEY

MIDFIELDER

Position: Forward **Date of Birth:** 28 April 1994
Place of Birth: Kidderminster **England Debut:** 19 October 2017 v France (A)

Able to perform in midfield or attack, Melissa Lawley made her senior debut for Arsenal in a UEFA Women's Champions League match against FK Bobruichanka in 2011 prior to a transfer to Bristol Academy the following year. An impressive three-year spell at Birmingham City came before Lawley's transfer to Manchester City in 2016, where she won two Women's FA Cups and the FA Women's Continental League Cup. The player, who had made over ten England appearances to date, was on the move again in 2019, signing for Liverpool.

ELLEN WHITE

FORWARD

Position: Forward **Date of Birth:** 09 May 1989
Place of Birth: Aylesbury **England Debut:** 25 March 2010 v Austria (H)

Ellen's performances at the 2019 FIFA Women's World Cup will live long in the memory, as she was joint-top goal-scorer at the tournament alongside the United States' Megan Rapinoe and Alex Morgan with six strikes in as many matches. The Manchester City forward netted on her Lionesses debut against Austria in March 2010 and marked her first appearance at FIFA Women's World Cup by scoring an audacious lob against eventual tournament winners Japan in 2011. She has twice been named England Senior Women's Player of the Year in both 2011 and 2018.

TONI DUGGAN

FORWARD

Position: Forward **Date of Birth:** 25 July 1991
Place of Birth: Liverpool **England Debut:** 18 September 2012 v Croatia (H)

Toni was a key member of Mo Marley's Young Lionesses squad that won the UEFA Women's U19 Championship back in 2009. The forward scored four goals as England won the competition for the first time. Toni was also capped at U17, U20 and U23 level as a youngster prior to making her senior debut in a 3-0 win over Croatia in September 2012. She has made over 75 international appearances since then and scored many important goals for her country, including hat-tricks against Turkey in September 2013 and Montenegro in April 2014.

BETHANY ENGLAND

FORWARD

Position: Forward **Date of Birth:** 03 June 1994
Place of Birth: Barnsley **England Debut:** 29 August 2019 v Belgium (A)

Bearing the perfect surname for a Lioness, Bethany represented her country at U19 and U23 level prior to her first senior call-up for England's back-to-back fixtures with Belgium and Norway in August 2019. Her first international goal came in a 2-1 defeat to Brazil at Middlesbrough's Riverside Stadium in October 2019 while she was on target a month later in a 3-2 triumph in the Czech Republic. Her 14 goals helped fire Chelsea to the Barclays FA WSL title in 2019/20.

LAUREN HEMP

FORWARD

Position: Forward **Date of Birth:** 07 August 2000
Place of Birth: North Walsham **England Debut:** 08 October 2019 v Portugal (A)

After making appearances for England at U17, U19, U20 and U21 level, Lauren has demonstrated her ability at senior international level in recent years, with her debut in 2019 followed by squad inclusion and two appearances at the 2020 SheBelieves Cup. The former Norwich City and Bristol City player, who was named as 2017/18 PFA Women's Young Player of the Year, joined Manchester City in 2018. She helped the Young Lionesses finish third at the FIFA U20 Women's World Cup that same year.

CHLOE KELLY

FORWARD

Position: Forward **Date of Birth:** 15 January 1998
Place of Birth: Hillingdon **England Debut:** 08 November 2018 v Austria (A)

Chloe has been included in a number of England squads since making her Lionesses' debut back in 2018. The forward travelled with Phil Neville's team to the 2020 SheBelieves Cup in the United States, where she featured in matches against the USA and Spain. She completed a transfer from Everton to Manchester City in the summer of 2020.

NIKITA PARRIS

FORWARD

Position: Forward **Date of Birth:** 10 March 1994
Place of Birth: Toxteth **England Debut:** 03 June 2016 v Serbia (H)

Sister of the boxer Natasha Jones, Nikita rose through the ranks at Everton – where she began her professional career – prior to transfers to Manchester City and Olympique Lyonnais. The 5ft 4" forward won her 50th England cap in the 1-0 SheBelieves Cup defeat to Spain in March 2020 having appeared in all seven of the Lionesses' matches at the FIFA Women's World Cup the previous year. Nikita scored 14 goals for England at the time of writing, with notable efforts including the winner against Portugal at UEFA Women's Euro 2017 and a strike against the United States in the successful 2019 SheBelieves Cup campaign.

BETH MEAD

FORWARD

Position: Forward **Date of Birth:** 09 May 1995
Place of Birth: Whitby **England Debut:** 06 April 2018 v Wales (H)

Beth played a crucial role in England's SheBelieves Cup success in 2019 as she netted in victories over Brazil and Japan. She was also in fine form at that summer's FIFA Women's World Cup, setting up three goals for her teammates during the tournament. The 2016 PFA Women's Young Player of the Year scored her eighth goal for her country in a 3-2 victory over Czech Republic in November 2019.

FRAN KIRBY

FORWARD

Position: Forward **Date of Birth:** 29 June 1993
Place of Birth: Reading **England Debut:** 02 August 2014 v Sweden (H)

2020 was a tough year for Fran, who had to spend a significant period on the sidelines through illness. The 2017/18 PFA and FWA Women's Players' Player of the Year will be hoping 2021 will see her back to full fitness and producing the kind of performances that saw her complete most key passes for England at the 2019 FIFA Women's World Cup, with eleven in total.

JODIE TAYLOR

FORWARD

Position: Forward **Date of Birth:** 17 May 1986
Place of Birth: Birkenhead **England Debut:** 03 August 2014 v Sweden (H)

Jodie Taylor has been a regular source of goals for England over the years, with her first strikes in a Lionesses' shirt coming in a 3-0 victory over Australia at the 2015 Cyprus Cup – a game in which she scored a hat-trick. She netted five times at UEFA Women's Euro 2017 - including a hat-trick in a 6-0 triumph over Scotland in Utrecht – to land the tournament's Golden Boot while her 18th international goal gave the Lionesses a 1-0 Group D win over Argentina at the 2019 FIFA Women's World Cup.

WOMEN'S SENIOR TEAM TOP TENS

TEN MOST CAPPED ENGLAND WOMEN'S SENIOR TEAM PLAYERS OF ALL-TIME

	PLAYER	ENGLAND CAREER	CAPS	GOALS
1st	Fara Williams	2001-to date	170	40
2nd	Jill Scott	2006–to date	149	24
3rd	Karen Carney	2005–2019	144	32
4th	Alex Scott	2004–2017	140	12
5th	Casey Stoney	2000–2018	130	6
6th	Rachel Yankey	1997–2013	129	19
7th	Steph Houghton	2007–to date	120	13
8th	Gillian Coultard	1981–2000	119	30
9th	Kelly Smith	1995–2014	117	46
Joint 10th	Rachel Unitt	2000-2013	102	8
Joint 10th	Eniola Aluko	2004–2016	102	33

TEN MOST PROLIFIC ENGLAND WOMEN'S SENIOR TEAM GOALSCORERS OF ALL-TIME

	PLAYER	ENGLAND CAREER	CAPS	GOALS
1st	Kelly Smith	1995–2014	117	46
2nd	Kerry Davis	1982–1998	82	44
Joint 3rd	Karen Walker	1988–2003	33	40
Joint 3rd	Fara Williams	2001- to date	170	40
5th	Ellen White	2010- to date	92	36
6th	Hope Powell	1983–1998	66	35
7th	Eniola Aluko	2004-2016	102	33
8th	Karen Carney	2005-2019	144	32
9th	Gillian Coultard	1981-2000	119	30
10th	Marieanne Spacey	1984–2001	91	28

(All information correct as of August 2020)

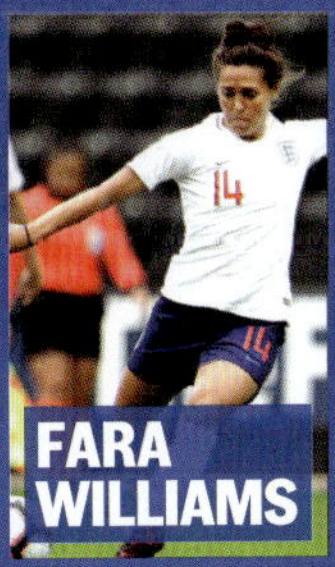

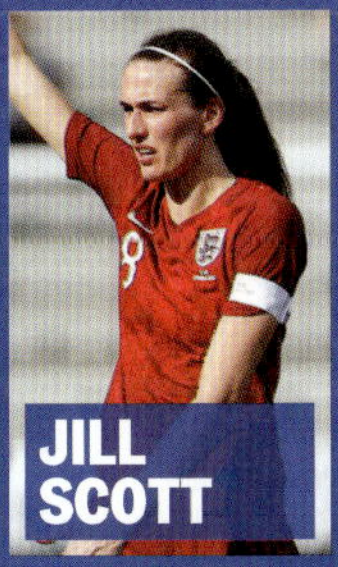

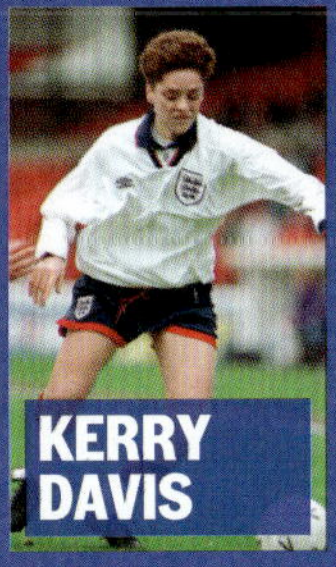

40 PLEDGE OF POSITIVITY

RESPECT OUR PLEDGE OF POSITIVITY

England skippers Steph Houghton and Harry Kane are backing The FA's Pledge of Positivity.

The FA launched the Pledge of Positivity in response to the findings of a survey (jointly conducted with Nielsen) that found 88 per cent of over 1000 grassroots football participants in England cite parents as a driver of disrespect.

England captains Steph Houghton and Harry Kane became the first people to take the Pledge back in February 2020, which urges parents and spectators involved in the grassroots game at Under-18 level to create a more positive environment at matches across the country.

The Pledge of Positivity reads;

As part of their support for the Pledge of Positivity campaign, Harry and Steph wrote a joint letter to parents and spectators, which was subsequently painted into the pitch touchlines of their former clubs - Ridgeway Rovers in Essex and Boldon Girls in South Shields – ahead of a round of youth team matches. The letter highlighted the importance positive support played in Harry and Steph's footballing development from grassroots football to international level.

LEAD BY EXAMPLE

CREATE THE RIGHT ENVIRONMENT

BUILD A POSITIVE TEAM AROUND YOU

UNDERSTAND YOUR PLAYERS

'ANYTHING IS POSSIBLE'

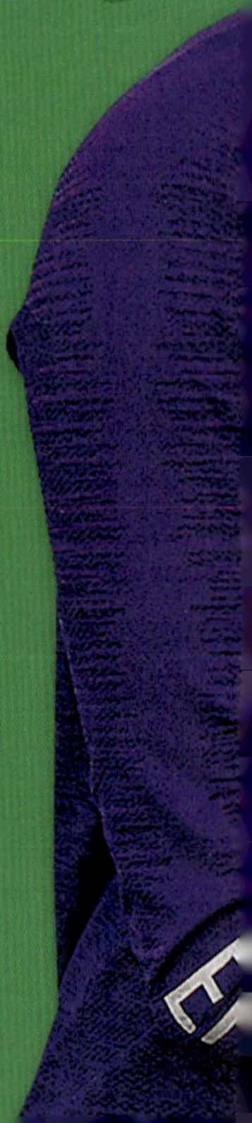

"As parents and spectators, it's our job to make sure that children enjoy playing football," wrote Kane, a father of two. "The pitch should be a place of support and encouragement. Youngsters should never feel pressure or intimidation from the sidelines, so I'm delighted to add my name to the Pledge of Positivity and I'd like to encourage as many people as possible to do the same."

And Lionesses captain Houghton added, "Positivity is essential in football. It's important to create an environment where everyone enjoys playing. There are small things you can do on the touchline – like applauding good play from both teams – that has a big impact on young players."

The Pledge is based on The FA's RESPECT behavioural code of conduct, which seeks to improve behavioural standards in football. The RESPECT campaign was re-launched ahead of the 2018/19 season, with a new mantra of 'We Only Do Positive'. The campaign was originally launched in 2008/09.

In 2018/19, positivity in grassroots football rose 88 per cent in tracked U12-U18s matches - a two per cent increase from the previous season. The FA hope that the Pledge of Positivity will ensure that number continues to rise.

42 COLOUR THE FLAGS

Can you correctly colour each of the following national flags of countries England could face at UEFA Euro 2020?

AUSTRIA

BELGIUM

CROATIA

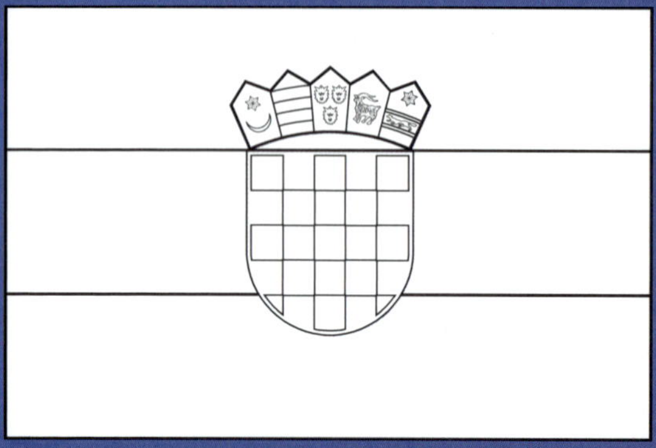

CZECH REPUBLIC

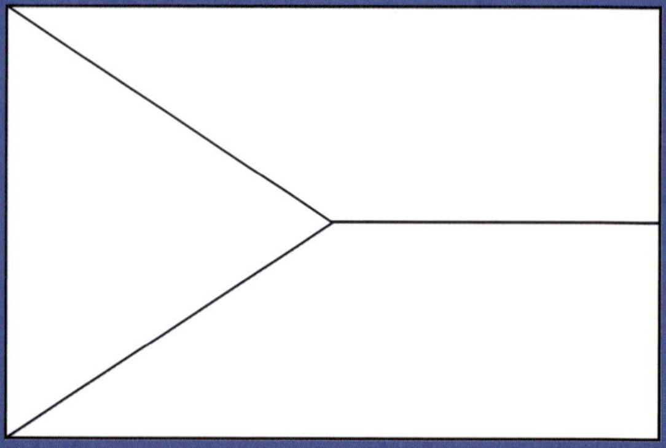

DENMARK

FINLAND

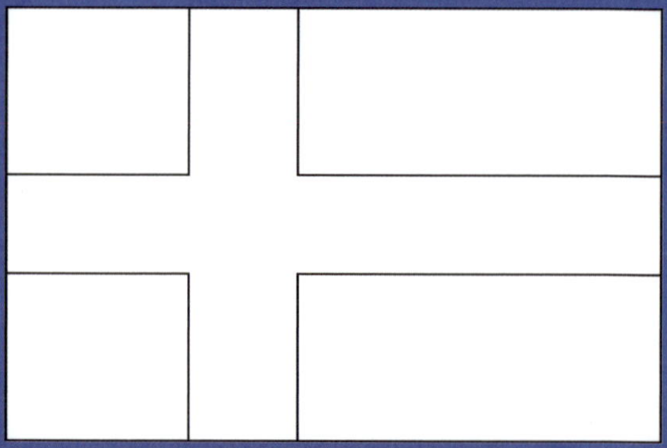

FRANCE

ITALY

POLAND

NETHERLANDS

RUSSIA

SWEDEN

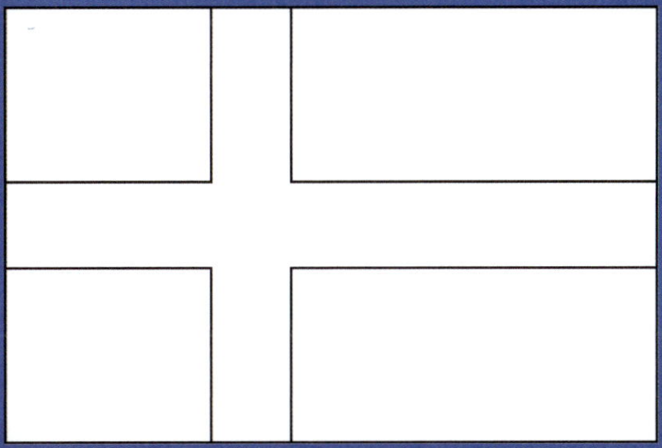

SWITZERLAND

TURKEY

Answers on page 60-61.

BT ENGLAND PLAYER OF THE YEAR AWARDS

After a year in which both players excelled with the England national team and won the UEFA Champions League with their respective clubs, Jordan Henderson and Lucy Bronze were named as the 2019 BT England Players of the Year.

Jordan Henderson

Jordan secured the Men's Senior accolade ahead of Raheem Sterling and Harry Kane, who finished second and third respectively in the voting. The Liverpool midfielder played seven times for England during 2019, winning his 50th cap for his country in the 5-1 away win in Montenegro in March that year. He was a pivotal figure in Gareth Southgate's squad during the year, which achieved qualification to UEFA Euro 2020 and also finished third in the inaugural UEFA Nations League finals.

The Sunderland-born player was named third in the vote for 'Midfielder of the Season' for 2018/19 at the UEFA Club Awards after a campaign in which he skippered Liverpool to glory in the UEFA Champions League, UEFA Super Cup and FIFA Club World Cup.

Lucy Bronze

Lucy won the Women's Senior Player of the Year award for a second time, having previously claimed the accolade in 2015. She finished ahead of 2018 winner Ellen White and Beth Mead in the vote to come out on top again in 2019. The Northumberland-raised defender played in 18 of England's 20 fixtures during the year, as the Lionesses lifted the SheBelieves Cup for the first time and reached the FIFA Women's World Cup semi-finals. For her efforts in the latter tournament, she was awarded with the Silver Ball.

At club level, Lucy helped Olympique Lyonnais win four major trophies in 2019 - the UEFA Women's Champions League, the Division 1 Féminine, the Coupe de France Féminine and the Trophée des Championnes – while she became the first English footballer to be named as the UEFA Women's Player of the Year Award.

GETTING SHIRTY!

Let's take a look at some of the classic England shirt designs over the years. Do you have a favourite?

BOBBY MOORE

Away - Year(s) in Use: 1965-74

England wore this classic, unbranded, crew-neck design shirt on eight different occasions between 1965 and 1974. Sir Alf Ramsey's Three Lions took to the Wembley pitch in it for the FIFA World Cup Final on 30 July 1966, which saw them beat West Germany 4-2 after extra-time in English football's finest hour.

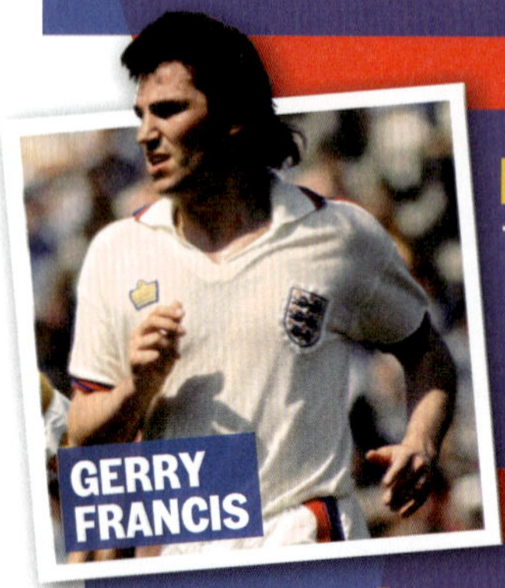
GERRY FRANCIS

Home - Year(s) in Use: 1974-80

The 1974-80 home design, which featured coloured stripes on the shoulders, arms, sleeves and collar, also incorporated a manufacturers' logo for the first time on a Three Lions shirt. This shirt was worn in 44 senior internationals, making its debut in a 3-0 victory over the former Czechoslovakia at Wembley Stadium in October 1974.

Away - Year(s) in Use: 1976-81

The bold design of the 1974-80 home shirt was mirrored by the away number, which was worn on 11 occasions by the Men's Senior team. The shirt design was slightly altered between 1976 and 1981, with tweaks such as the colours used on the manufacturers' logo being swapped.

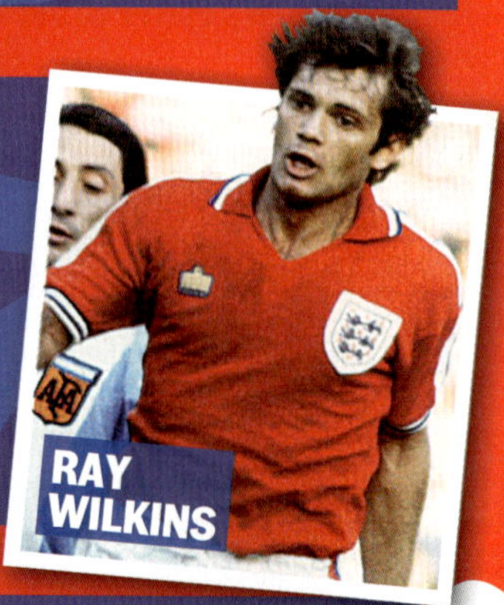
RAY WILKINS

TREVOR FRANCIS

Home - Year(s) in Use: 1981-83

England first wore this eye-catching home shirt for a 3-1 triumph over world champions Argentina at Wembley in May 1980. The shirt was also worn at the 1982 FIFA World Cup, with lightweight versions issued to Three Lions players for matches against Kuwait and Spain at the tournament due to the hot conditions. Its final appearance in a senior match came in a goalless draw with Greece in March 1983.

Home - Year(s) in Use: 1984-87

This classic home shirt, with its striking V-neck collar, was worn in five matches at the 1986 FIFA World Cup, including a 3-0 victory over Poland that saw Gary Lineker score a hat-trick. On a number of occasions, including matches against Brazil and Chile in 1984, white shorts were worn instead of the default royal blue ones due to kit clashes.

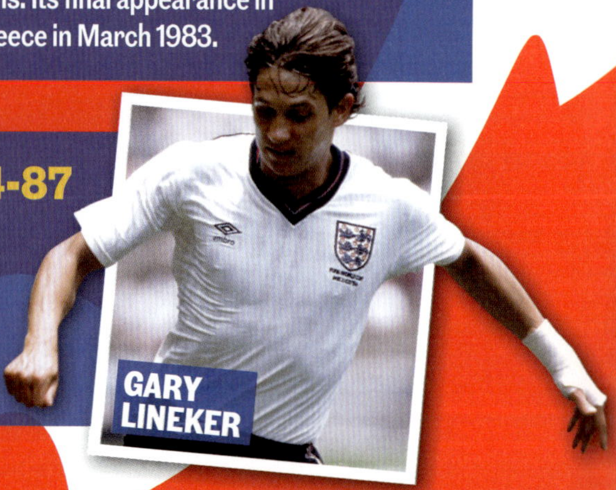
GARY LINEKER

Home - Year(s) in Use: 1990-92

The 1990-92 England home shirt will forever be synonymous with the Three Lions' heroic performances at the 1990 FIFA World Cup and Paul Gascoigne's tears after receiving a yellow card in the semi-final match with West Germany. The shirt was worn in 31 senior internationals between March 1990 and November 1992 with its last outing coming in a 4-0 victory over Turkey in a 1994 FIFA World Cup qualifier.

PAUL GASCOIGNE

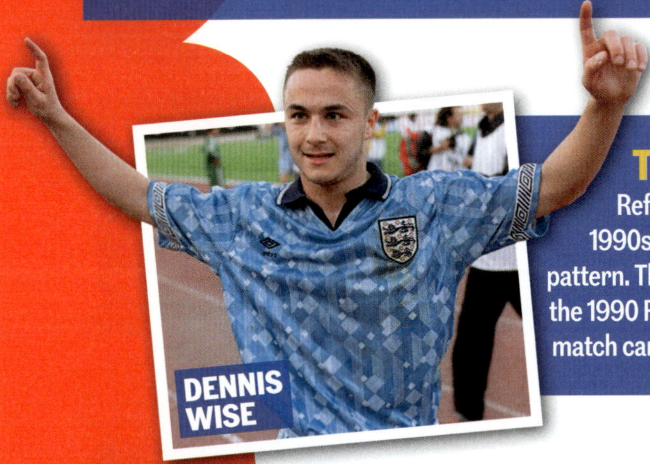
DENNIS WISE

Third - Year(s) in Use: 1990-91

Reflecting the gaudy trend of football shirts during the 1990s, this pale blue number features a multi-layered shadow pattern. The third shirt was issued but never worn by England at the 1990 FIFA World Cup. Indeed, its only outing in a Men's Senior match came in a 1-0 away victory in Turkey in May 1991.

Third - Year(s) in Use: 1992

Similar in colour to its predecessor - but featuring three huge lions in a darker blue hue on a pale blue background - this third shirt was twice worn by England in 1992 in away matches against Czechoslovakia and Spain.

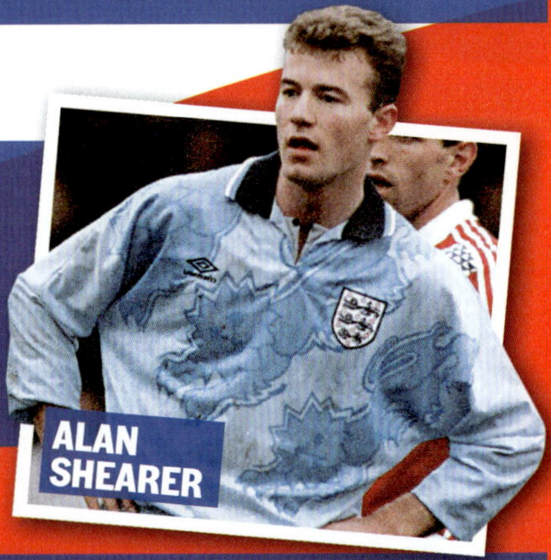
ALAN SHEARER

STUART PEARCE

Home - Year(s) in Use: 1995-96

This classic England home shirt evokes memories of UEFA Euro 1996. The Three Lions wore it in four tournament matches en route a semi-final showdown with Germany. Both David Baddiel and Frank Skinner sported the shirt in the official music video for Three Lions (Football's Coming Home) – a song they co-wrote with Ian Broudie and performed with the Lightning Seeds.

Away - Year(s) in Use: 1996

Officially classed as 'indigo blue' - although grey in the eyes of many – England wore this away shirt in their UEFA Euro 1996 semi-final match against Germany, which ended in a heart-breaking penalty shoot-out defeat for Terry Venables' side. The shirt was also worn in a 1-0 friendly victory over Bulgaria in March 1996 and a 2-0 FIFA World Cup qualifying victory in Georgia later that year.

TEDDY SHERINGHAM

Home - Year(s) in Use: 1997-99

One of the greatest individual goals in English football was scored in this shirt by a certain 18-year-old by the name of Michael Owen against Argentina at the 1998 FIFA World Cup. England won the 1997 Tournoi de France tournament in this shirt and booked their place at the following year's World Cup in the same design, when they secured a goalless draw against Italy in Rome in October 1997.

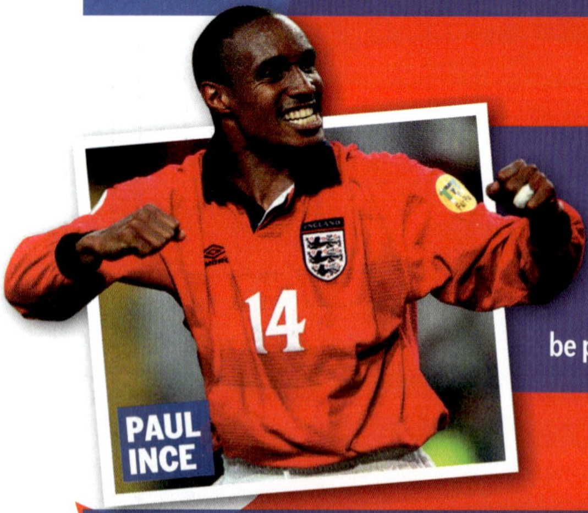

Away - Year(s) in Use: 1999-2001

England wore this attractive red shirt in their 1-0 win over Germany at UEFA Euro 2000, while it was also their chosen outfit for the 1-0 defeat to the same opponents in the last-ever match to be played at the 'old' Wembley Stadium in October 2000.

Home - Year(s) in Use: 2001-03

Another of England's great goals was scored in this shirt, which was launched on St. George's Day 2001. David Beckham's 30-yard, curling free-kick in stoppage time at the end of the 90 minutes secured a 2-2 draw with Greece and with it the Three Lions' place at the 2002 FIFA World Cup.

Away - Year(s) in Use: 2006-08

Speaking of great goals, Joe Cole's long-range volley in a 2-2 draw with Sweden at the 2006 FIFA World Cup was scored in this red away shirt. The shirt featured a golden star above the Three Lions crest, to honour the 40th anniversary of England's World Cup triumph in 1966. The players also wore golden lettering and numbers on this shirt.

Away - Year(s) in Use: 2008

England launched a new away kit in February 2008, which once again featured a red shirt. A QR code was included on the shirt's label – believed to be the first time a football shirt had ever incorporated such technology. The Three Lions first wore the shirt in a 2-1 friendly win over Switzerland while the last of its five outings in a Men's Senior game came in the 2-1 victory in Germany in November 2008.

Home - Year(s) in Use: 2009-10

The 2009/10 home shirt was created using a bespoke tailoring process for each player. The stylish, made-to-measure kit – which was sold to supporters by chest size rather than the conventional 'small', 'medium', 'large' etc – was worn in matches against USA and Algeria at the 2010 FIFA World Cup.

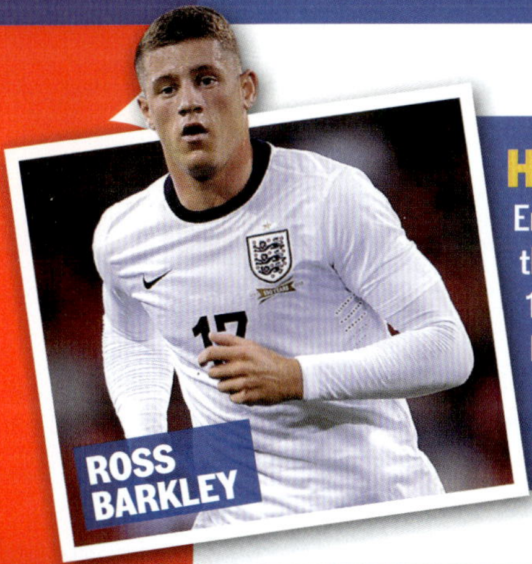

Home - Year(s) in Use: 2013-14

England's first-ever home shirt manufactured by Nike celebrated the 150th anniversary of the FA, which was founded on 26 October 1863. The round-neck design was worn for the first time in the Three Lions 1-1 draw with the Republic of Ireland at Wembley Stadium in May 2013 and had its last outing in a 1-0 victory over Denmark at the same venue in March 2014.

Home - Year(s) in Use: 2018-20

This traditional-looking yet contemporary home shirt was worn in three England matches at the 2018 FIFA World Cup, including the 2-1 extra-time defeat to Croatia in the semi-final of the tournament. It was also used in the Three Lions' successful UEFA Nations League campaign in 2018/19, that saw Gareth Southgate's men beat the likes of Croatia and Spain to top their group and reach the finals of the competition.

Away - Year(s) in Use: 2018-20

This away shirt will be remembered for England's first triumph in a FIFA World Cup penalty shootout. Harry Kane, Marcus Rashford, Kieran Trippier and Eric Dier all netted from the spot in this classic red number as the Three Lions beat Colombia 4-3 on spot-kicks after their round of 16 match had finished 1-1 after extra-time. after extra-time

Away - Year(s) in Use: 2019-Present

For the first time ever, England's Women's Senior team had two exclusive kits produced for their appearance at the 2019 FIFA World Cup. The away number was an articulation of England's classic red away strip. Rendered in a 'dark red crush', the shirt featured a custom hand-drawn print highlighting specific flora native to England and a tonal crest unique to the Lionesses. It was worn in the 1-0 victory over Argentina at the tournament, which saw Jodie Taylor score the winning goal.

HEALTHY MEALS
EAT LIKE A PRO!

Here are some handy tips to help you eat a healthy, balanced diet like your Three Lions and Lionesses heroes.

Get Your Five a Day!

Fruit and vegetables are an important source of vitamins and minerals - including folate, vitamin C and potassium. The World Health Organization (WHO) recommends we all eat five portions of fruit and veg every day (that's five portions in total, not five equal portions of each). For adults, each portion is 80g, while for children, a portion is roughly the amount you can get in your hand – which grows in size as you do!

Fruit and veg are an excellent source of fibre, which can help maintain a healthy gut and prevent digestion problems. Some footballers look to eat certain 'super' fruit and vegetables, that are particularly packed with vitamins, minerals and antioxidants. Sweet potatoes, for example, are rich in beta-Carotene, which helps protect vision. Raspberries meanwhile are high in fibre, which helps maintain regular bowel movement.

One of the keys to a healthy, balance diet is to eat as many different fruits and vegetables as you can during the course of a week.

Start the Day Right

Breakfast has traditionally been described as the 'most important meal of the day' and whether you've got a busy day lined-up at school or on the training pitch, it's vital to give your body the fuel it needs.

England skipper Harry Kane likes to start his days with an omelette, a slice of brown toast and a side of spinach. Eggs are great source of protein, while brown bread in an excellent form of carbohydrate. Like many dark green vegetables, spinach helps reduced blood pressure and its packed full of various vitamins and minerals.

Cereals are another good source of carbs and fortified cereals have certain vitamins and minerals added to them. Just be careful to avoid ones that are high in sugar, fat or salt.

Keep it Balanced!

A well-balanced diet should contain a good range of protein such as fresh meat, fish, peas, beans, nuts, seeds and meat alternatives, as well as carbohydrates like rice, cereal, potatoes, pasta and rice. It should be high in fibre and low in saturated fat, sugar and salt and ideally containing plenty of milk and dairy products, like cheese and yoghurt.

Lionesses skipper Steph Houghton often starts her day with a boiled egg and smoked salmon, while she is a big fan of chicken and salad for lunch. One of her regular dinnertime meals is salmon with lots of vegetables, including sweet potato.

Prepare Well on Matchday!

On a game day, it is extra important to eat an appropriate amount of protein and carbohydrate-rich foods to fuel you for the game. Players usually eat a number of hours before kick-off or training, to avoid feeling heavy going out onto the pitch.

England players Kyle Walker and Fran Kirby both like to eat spaghetti bolognese on the day of a game. Walker's chef has revealed a particularly healthy twist – cooking the defender's pasta in beetroot juice so it absorbs the vegetable's iron and nitrates to give Walker an extra boost before kick-off!

Keep Hydrated!

Drinking plenty of water is vital to help ensure the regular functioning of bodies. The European Food Safety Authority (EFSA) recommends that 4-to 8-year-olds should drink between 1.1 and 1.3 litres per day while 9-to-13-year-old girls should up their fluids to 1.3 to 1.5 litres and 9-to-13-year-old boys to rough 1.5 to 1.7 litres on a daily basis. Roughly 70-80 of our fluid comes from drinks, the rest from food.

52 ST. GEORGE'S PARK

Opened back in 2012, St. George's Park is home to all 28 England national teams.

The Football Association's National Football Centre (NFC), St. George's Park, was officially opened by the Duke and Duchess of Cambridge on 9 October 2012. Set in 330-acres of Staffordshire countryside, the centre is the base for all of England's national teams including the Men's Senior and Women's Senior squads.

The facility was designed by Alan J Smith OBE's Red Box Design Group, who were also behind projects such as Sunderland Aquatic Centre, Sunderland AFC's Academy of Light, and Durham County Cricket Club's Emirates Riverside Ground in Chester-le-Street.

The St. George's Park site incorporates 13 outdoor pitches, including one – the Sir Bobby Charlton pitch – that is an exact replica of the Wembley playing surface. There is also a full-size indoor 3G pitch and futsal arena, as well as a suite of rehabilitation and sports science areas.

Futsal Arena

Sir Bobby Charlton Pitch

St. George's Park is the home of FA Education and delivers all FA national coach education courses. The range of courses - covering a variety of disciplines - are aligned to the England DNA philosophy, consisting of five core elements with the long-term aim to produce winning England teams at senior level.

There is an Outdoor Leadership Centre on-site, which delivers development programmes in the areas of leadership, management and team building, while there is also a 228-bedroom Hotel.

England's various national teams train at St. George's Park prior to international fixtures while countless professional club sides from around the world including Barcelona, Galatasaray, Monaco and Minnesota United have used its facilities over the years. St. George's Park staged five group stage matches during the 2018 UEFA U17 Championships, when England would go on to suffer a cruel penalty shoot-out defeat in the semi-final against the Netherlands.

SGP Gym

Full-size indoor 3G pitch

WORDSEARCH

Find the surnames of some of England Men's Senior and Women's Senior teams' record appearance makers.

Y	M	H	T	I	M	S	R	M	S	U	N	I	T	T
J	A	R	O	B	S	O	N	L	C	N	Y	Y	H	M
Y	N	N	D	D	F	T	M	H	O	Y	D	G	A	R
F	E	K	K	X	K	R	O	Q	T	Y	I	H	J	L
L	X	N	C	E	R	Q	K	V	T	R	K	M	M	T
J	R	L	O	H	Y	M	U	G	W	C	E	P	C	S
T	W	O	T	T	A	K	L	M	E	R	M	O	H	K
C	K	N	O	N	S	R	A	B	O	W	U	I	S	R
O	W	L	O	N	R	D	L	O	T	L	L	D	M	K
L	F	T	D	T	E	Z	M	T	T	T	K	R	A	Q
E	X	Y	K	N	H	Y	Y	A	O	Q	B	A	I	L
C	A	R	N	E	Y	G	R	N	N	N	R	P	L	T
G	R	B	K	P	M	D	U	D	N	L	M	M	L	N
M	D	R	A	R	R	E	G	O	Y	G	Q	A	I	R
C	L	P	F	R	T	J	F	V	H	R	L	L	W	Z

ALUKO
BECKHAM
CARNEY
CHARLTON
COLE
COULTARD
GERRARD
HOUGHTON
LAMPARD
MOORE
ROBSON
ROONEY
SCOTT
SHILTON
SMITH
STONEY
WILLIAMS
WRIGHT
UNITT
YANKEY

Answers on page 60-61.

FILL IN THE BLANKS

Fill in the gaps in information that appear over these two pages...

WHO AM I?!

Look at the profile information below and fill in the missing names of these Men's Senior and Women's Senior Team players...

Men's Senior Team Players

1
Position: Goalkeeper
Date of Birth: 07 March 1994
Place of Birth: Washington
England Debut: 10 November 2017 v Germany (H)

Who am I?!

2
Position: Defender
Date of Birth: 28 May 1994
Place of Birth: Barnsley
England Debut: 30 May 2014 v Peru (H)

Who am I?!

3
Position: Midfielder
Date of Birth: 11 April 1996
Place of Birth: Milton Keynes
England Debut: 09 October 2015 v Estonia (H)

Who am I?!

4
Position: Forward
Date of Birth: 31 October 1997
Place of Birth: Manchester
England Debut: 27 May 2016 v Australia (H)

Who am I?!

Women's Senior Team Players

5
Position: Goalkeeper
Date of Birth: 23 September 1999
Place of Birth: Sheffield
England Debut: 08 November 2018 v Austria (A)

Who am I?!

6
Position: Defender
Date of Birth: 28 October 1991
Place of Birth: Berwick-upon-Tweed
England Debut: 26 June 26 2013 v Japan (H)

Who am I?!

7
Position: Defender
Date of Birth: March 29, 1997
Place of Birth: Milton Keynes
England Debut: June 8, 2018 v Russia (A)

Who am I?!

8
Position: Forward
Date of Birth: 25 July 1991
Place of Birth: Liverpool
England Debut: 19 September 2012 v Croatia (H)

Who am I?!

WHAT'S THE SCORE?

Can you fill in the scoreboards from these European Championship matches?

1 UEFA Euro 1996
Group A
15 June 1996

England	
Scotland	

2 UEFA Euro 2000
Group A
17 June 2000

England	
Germany	

3 UEFA Euro 2004
Group B
17 June 2004

England	
Switzerland	

4 UEFA Euro 2004
Group B
21 June 2004

England	
Croatia	

5 UEFA Euro 2012
Group D
15 June 2012

England	
Sweden	

6 UEFA Euro 2012
Group B
16 June 2016

England	
Wales	

ON TARGET

Name the missing goal scorers from these UEFA Euro 2020 qualifying matches.

RESULT	GOALSCORER(S)
1 Wembley Stadium, London, 22 March 2019	
England 5	____________ 24', 62', 68', Kane 45+2' (pen.), Kalas (o.g) 84'
Czech Republic 0	–
2 City Stadium, Podgorica, 25 March 2019	
Montenegro 1	Vesovic 17'
England 5	Keane 30' ____________ 39', 59', Kane 71', Sterling 81'
3 Wembley Stadium, London, 07 September 2019	
England 4	____________ 24', 50' (pen.), 73' (pen.), Sterling 55'
Bulgaria 0	–
4 Wembley Stadium, London, 10 September 2019	
England 5	Sterling 8', Kane 19', Vojvoda (o.g.) 38', ____________ 44', 45+1'
Kosovo 3	V.Berisha 1', 49', Muriqi (pen.)
5 Vasil Levski National Stadium, Sofia, 14 October 2019	
Bulgaria 0	–
England 6	____________ 7', Barkley 20', 32', Sterling 45+3', Kane 85'
6 Wembley Stadium, London, 14 November 2019	
England 7	____________ 11', Kane 19',24',37', Rashford 30', Sofranac (o.g.) 66' ____________ 84'
Montenegro 0	–

Answers on page 60-61.

BIG ENGLAND QUIZ

1. In which country was England striker Raheem Sterling born in 1994?

2. Who is the All-Time Most Capped Player for the Three Lions?

3. Who were the Lionesses' first-ever opponents back in November 1972?

4. Which Barclays FA WSL club team do Leah Williamson and Jordan Nobbs play for?

5. Against which country did manager Gareth Southgate make his managerial debut for England?

6. Who were the first England players to take the FA's Pledge of Positivity in February 2020?

7. Which England defender scored two goals against Panama at the 2018 FIFA World Cup?

8. Who is the Three Lions assistant coach?

9. By what scoreline did England beat Sweden at UEFA Euro 2008?

10. In which city were Alex Greenwood and Ross Barkley born in 1993?

11. In the 2018 FIFA World Cup round of 16 penalty shoot-out against Colombia, who scored England's winning spot-kick?

12. Which nations did England face in the 2019 UEFA Nations League finals?

13. Which teams did the Lionesses beat on the way to victory in the 2019 SheBelieves Cup?

14. Who became the youngest-ever player to feature in a senior competitive match for the Three Lions when he was introduced as a substitute in a 5-0 win over the Czech Republic in March 2019 at the age of just 18 years and 135 days?

15. What year did England first appear at the finals of a European Championships?

16. Who were England U21s' opponents in the first-ever match to be staged at Wembley Stadium in March 2007?

17. Who won the BT England Men's Senior Player of the Year in 2019?

18. Who won the BT England Women's Senior Player of the Year in 2019?

19. Which Lionesses striker was the joint-top goal-scorer at the 2019 FIFA Women's World Cup with the United States' forwards Megan Rapinoe and Alex Morgan?

20. Which of England's UEFA Euro 2020 Group D opponents did the Three Lions also face at the 2018 FIFA World Cup?

Answers on page 60-61.

CROSSWORD

ACROSS

2 Training base for England's 24 national teams. (2,7,4)

3 Shirt colour worn by England in their 1996 FIFA World Cup Final triumph over West Germany. (3)

4 The Lionesses' most capped player of all time - Fara ________. (8)

5 England's current kit manufacturer. (4)

8 The anthem sung before England matches. (3,4,3,5)

10 Abbreviation for Video Assistant Referee. (3)

11 Opponents England beat 7-0 at Wembley Stadium in November 2019 to book a place at UEFA Euro 2020. (10)

DOWN

1 England striker Kevin Oghenetega Bakumo-Abraham is best known by the name _____ (5)

2 Scored two goals in England's 4-1 win over the Netherlands at UEFA Euro 1996 - Teddy __________. (10)

6 Scored two goals in England's 4-1 win over the Netherlands at UEFA Euro 1996 - Alan _______. (7)

7 Number of UEFA Euro 2000 matches that will be staged at Wembley Stadium. (5)

9 The Lionesses' record, all-time goal scorer - Kelly _____. (5)

Answers on page 60-61.

NATIONAL ANTHEM

Sing along to the national anthem prior to England matches!

GOD SAVE THE QUEEN

God save our gracious Queen!

Long live our noble Queen!

God save the Queen!

Send her victorious,
Happy and glorious,
Long to reign over us:
God save the Queen!

QUIZ AND PUZZLE ANSWERS

PAGES 42-43: COLOUR THE FLAGS

AUSTRIA

ITALY

CROATIA

POLAND

BELGIUM

NETHERLANDS

CZECH REPUBLIC

RUSSIA

DENMARK

SWEDEN

FINLAND

SWITZERLAND

FRANCE

TURKEY

PAGE 53: WORDSEARCH

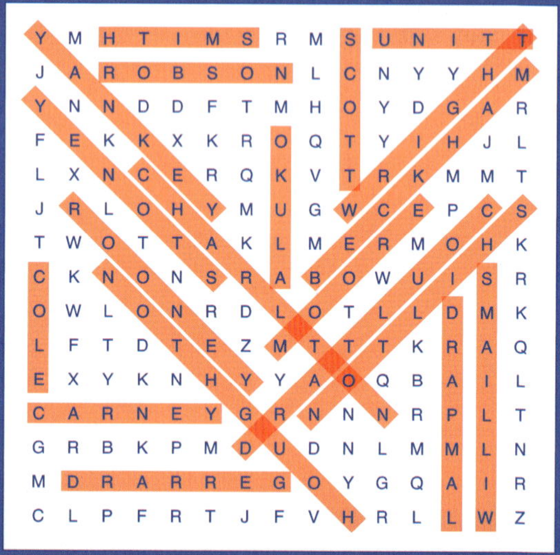

PAGES 54-55: FILL IN THE BLANKS WHO AM I?!

1. Jordan Pickford
2. John Stones
3. Dele Alli
4. Marcus Rashford
5. Ellie Roebuck
6. Lucy Bronze
7. Leah Williamson
8. Toni Duggan

WHAT'S THE SCORE?

1	England	2
	Scotland	0
2	England	1
	Germany	0
3	England	3
	Switzerland	0
4	England	4
	Croatia	2
5	England	3
	Sweden	2
6	England	2
	Wales	1

ON TARGET

1. STERLING
2. BARKLEY
3. KANE
4. SANCHO
5. RASHFORD
6. OXLADE-CHAMBERLAIN, ABRAHAM

PAGE 56: QUIZ

1. Jamaica
2. Peter Shilton - 125
3. Scotland
4. Arsenal
5. Malta
6. Harry Kane & Steph Houghton
7. John Stones
8. Steve Holland
9. 3-2
10. Liverpool
11. Eric Dier
12. Netherlands & Switzerland
13. Brazil & Japan
14. Callum Hudson-Odoi
15. 1968
16. Italy U21s
17. Jordan Henderson
18. Lucy Bronze
19. Ellen White
20. Croatia

PAGE 57: CROSSWORD

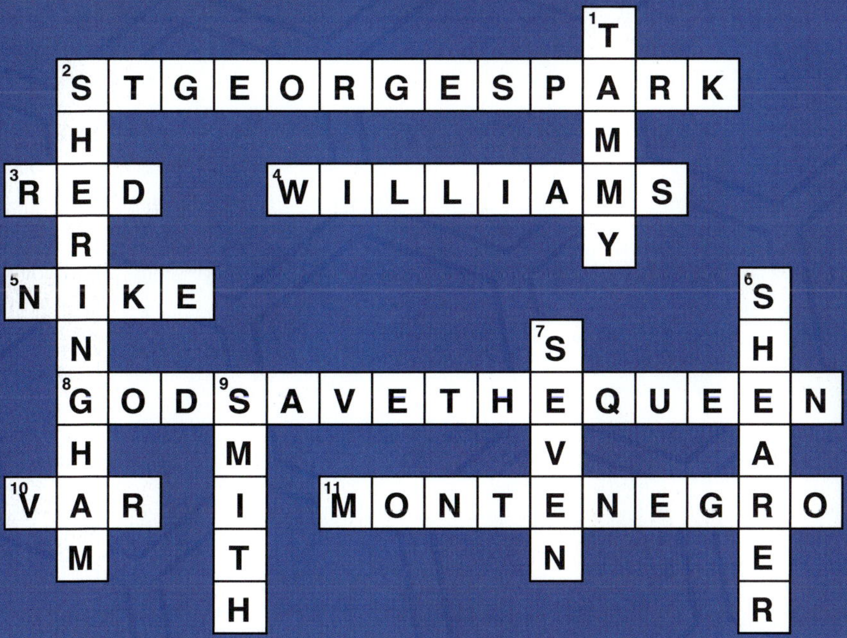

62 SPOT THE PLAYERS

Can you spot the five Lions and Lionesses hiding in the crowd?